You're Hired!

Interview Skills to Get the Job
By Lorne Epstein

2nd Edition
E3 Publishing • Arlington, Virginia

Published by:
E3 Publishing

Orders@yourehiredbook.com
http://www.YoureHiredBook.com

You're Hired! Interview Skills to Get the Job by Lorne Epstein
2nd ed.

ISBN: 0-9760632-0-4

Printed 2007

Cover photography: Michael Billewicz, Gotcha Photography
Models: Alicia Korten, Adam Brook, Lorne Epstein
Editor: Deidre Gantt, Phenom
Cover and interior design: Brenda McVeigh
Typeset in Garamond Pro

Printed in the United States of America

Acknowledgements

I want to thank all of the people who have taken great effort and made a significant contribution to who I have become.

I thank God for the inspiration and resources to accomplish this goal. She has been a great friend and helper along my journey.

I am thankful for my love, Alicia.

I thank my parents, Diana Epstein and Martin Epstein, who always believed in my ability to succeed and gave me everything I needed to reach my goals.

To my brother, Daniel Epstein, who is a good friend and the best brother I could ask for.

To my sister, Sara Epstein, who is a kind, independent, and brilliant thinker. I was fortunate enough to have her as my first editor.

To those teachers who supported me in my formative years: Donald Delman, David Lelonek, Larry Leshay, Steven Sunshine, and Dr. Charles Canedy III.

To those who trained, coached, and influenced me to be my best: Terry Nelson, Lou Dozier, Charlene Afremow, Lisa Kalmin, Dr. Jorge Haddock, Dr. Joel Martin, and Neale Donald Walsh. And thanks to Alex Ferranti, who has been with me on my journey for many years.

To LP 81, LP 88, LP 115, OC 4, and all of the E3 graduates, I thank you for teaching me to listen, learn, and love.

To those friends who have supported me: Jennifer Barry, Dr. Andrew Catanzaro and Laura Elkins, Steven Dixel, Susan Holland, Elizabeth Phelps, Shelby Pierce, Joe and Amour Ross, Christine and Bill Tiernay.

To my principal editor and moral compass, Carol Cross, who has been a source of unconditional love and support in helping me with gentle commas all the way through to completion of this project.

To Brenda McVeigh, who did an outstanding job of getting the book to completion with her artistic talents.

To Michael "Rebbi Mike" Farber, who gave me my first break as a recruiter.

To Joy Yoshioka and all the HR and Hiring Managers who taught me well.

To the thousands of you who allowed me to support you in your job search, to you I give my appreciation and good wishes for making this book possible.

This book is dedicated to my grandparents
who came to this country,
struggled, served, and gave of themselves
to make a better future
for their children and children's children:

Max and Lillian Sussman

Eli and Dora Epstein

Listen

to

You're Hired Radio!

Lorne's podcast can be heard at iTunes.com

"You're Hired Radio" with Lorne Epstein entertains and informs you on issues relating to your Job and Career. Lorne shows you how to get a raise, how to interview, and how to get the job of your dreams. He covers issues from the perspectives of the employee and employer.

Table of Contents

Chapter 3: What to Do During the Interview

Chapter 4: What to Do After the Interview

Chapter 5: Conclusion

The Introduction

You are totally screwed every time you walk into an interview. You are outgunned and outmanned because you only interview once every several years, while your interviewers do this every day. This gives them an edge.

Or at least that may be what you believe!

You may think that when it comes to getting a job, interviewers have more power than you do. But this does not have to be true. You have more power in running your life and getting a job than they do. You may not get a particular job, which is okay because you are reading this to get a good job—the right job for you. In your town and across the country, there are hundreds of companies that value your skills.

I want to let you in on a little secret. People who are looking to hire someone want to make an offer sooner rather than later. The employer wants you to be "the one" who gets the job. They don't want to spend their time, money, and energy continually interviewing people to fill a position. They want to hire you and get back to the business of the organization. Your job is to get out of your own way so that by the end of the interview, the employers can feel comfortable fulfilling their desire to make you an offer.

That doesn't sound so bad, does it? Unfortunately, things don't always go so smoothly. I have conducted thousands of interviews, and believe me, I've seen the good, the bad, and the ugly. I have seen many good candidates not get hired simply because they foul up the process. They miss one good opportunity to seal the deal, like forgetting to send a thank you note to the right person at the right time.

The second secret I am going to let you in on is that your success hangs on your ability to ace the interview. In tight job markets, getting a good job is competitive, so honing your interviewing skills will give you the edge in seeking that magic offer letter. During the interview, you must use every tool at your disposal. There are many to choose from, including some you probably haven't thought of using. This book is a step-by-step approach to navigating the interview process and using the right tools to get an offer letter from a company that's right for you.

Who the Heck Am I?

You may be wondering why you should listen to me. You should listen to me because hiring people like you is what I do for a living. I am a professional recruiter—the guy who would be sitting across the table asking you questions if you ever applied for a job with one of my clients. Over the years, I have interviewed thousands and hired hundreds of people for various sizes and types of organizations.

I also know the job market from your perspective. As the owner of a consulting services business, I have had over 30 clients say to me "You're Hired!" I have experienced the hurdles that one can stumble upon, and I have surpassed them many times. In this book, I share the wisdom I have learned from being on both sides of the interview table. My unique perspective will help you see that the interview process is your greatest friend, not an enemy to be cursed when a job is not awarded to you.

My Commitment to You

I wrote this book and I do this work because I care about you and the life you lead. It matters to me that you are happy. I cannot explain why it matters; it just does. My concern for your success comes from my idealistic belief that if everyone on the planet was doing work that made him or her happy, we would all live in a better world.

I intend to take your fear away and replace it with some humor, good ideas, and *sachel* (this means common sense in Yiddish). Everyone can use a little *sachel* now and then.

Come to this book knowing nothing and
you will learn something about yourself.
Come knowing everything and you will
learn nothing.

I know that jobs are helpful in living life and paying bills. They also can provide a sense of accomplishment and joy. So whatever a job means to you, I honor that, and I honor your purpose in having one. I urge you to use this book to go forth and give the best interviews ever!

You just spent $15.00, and while that is not a lot of money, why not make that hard-earned dough-ray-me sing for you like Pavarotti at the opera?

Being Happy with Work

We tend to know little about things that are important to us and a lot about things that are insignificant to our heartfelt happiness. To test this notion, think back to the last time you argued with your lover, partner, spouse, or friend and had no clue what it was about. Now remember what day and time your favorite TV show starts.

Being happy in your career and the job you do is important. I am inviting you to raise your level of happiness in your career and your job.

You may find that you are not "happy" with the work that you do, but if you can increase your sense of satisfaction and joy, you are on the track to Right Livelihood. You spend 40 hours a week, 2080 hours a year, for 40 years (or more) doing this thing called a "job." That is a significant part of my life, and I want to make the most of it.

I choose to create Right Livelihood. I choose to leave everything I have on the playing field of life, knowing that I did everything I could to live my life's purpose and enjoy my time. I refuse to replace my happiness with prime-time television and an excuse that I am too busy, too unskilled, or too anything to live my life's purpose and raise my sense of accomplishment and joy. You are invited to bridge the gaps in creating your Right Livelihood.

About YOU!

If you are a "rain maker" attorney, this book is for you. If you are a physician, desk clerk (what is a desk clerk anyway?), hairdresser, sales professional, accountant, consultant, manager, computer programmer, mechanic, fireman, environmental activist, or C-level executive, this book is for you. Maybe not the entire book. Maybe only one chapter. But I can assure you that anyone, ANYONE who needs to interview for a job can use this book.

Since you bought this streamlined book and not some 500-page snoozer that costs more money, I will presume that you are thrifty and smart. Yes, you are very smart indeed. That is a great advantage in your job hunt. Being smarter than the average bear can make all the difference in the world. Being smarter means knowing more of what goes on in the hearts and minds of recruiters and hiring managers (and they can be a tricky lot).

About This Book

To help you with the interview process, *You're Hired!* is divided into three sections: what to DO before, during, and after the interview. In the first section, I help you to prepare for the interview. In the second section, I walk you through the interview, illuminating which questions to ask and which ones you shouldn't answer. I show you how to present yourself in a comprehensive way and how to glean the information you will need to make a clear decision when you get the offer. In the third section, I teach you how to follow up, and I reveal tricks you can use to seal the deal. Your interview will be most successful if you see the interview process as the sum of all three parts.

Consider what I have written here as an "apparel store" full of ideas that you can wear to get the job of your dreams. Now that you have bought the entire store, go ahead and try on everything to see what fits. You may judge, resist, or reject some of my advice. I would suggest to you that those very ideas are the ones you may want to try on. Do so and you will create a wonderful wardrobe of interviewing skills.

Clothing stores have a particular style, like The GAP or Old Navy, and so does my writing. I am not a writer telling you how to interview. I am sharing my first-hand experiences. I intend to make this book easy to read, as if you were right here next to me on my couch, listening to me speak. I write in a form that is colloquial to my upbringing in Brooklyn, New York.

I kept this book short to give you only the pearls you need. I want you to read it, refer to it, and use it to get better jobs more quickly. I believe that you will become a better candidate by using the information in this book.

I use the words recruiter and hiring manager to describe the roles of the people involved in your hiring process. For you, these terms refer to the person who finds candidates to fill the job and the person who chooses to hire those candidates, respectively.

Who Are You?

"Who am I?" Have you asked yourself this simple yet profound question? I dare you to ask yourself this right now. Your answers are at the heart of identifying the job or career that is right for you. Ask and hear what your answer is. Ask again and listen to what the voice in your mind says. Keep asking and notice whether your answer changes. Listen with your heart. Do your answers make sense to you once you hear them? Are they silly? Fun? Serious? Do they shake you to your core?

Remember to take time every now and again to ask yourself this question. It is a question designed to inspire a lifetime of self-exploration. If you meditate, this is a wonderful question to ponder.

If you still have not answered the question, don't fret. There is no finite answer, only the ever-changing, ever-evolving person that you will become. As you move through this process, you will become clearer about who you are. As your self-awareness increases, you will find yourself more able to choose a satisfying, enjoyable, and productive career.

Though this book is a step-by-step guide to interviewing, my overarching mission is to help you find a livelihood that fits you alone. When you have clarity about a job that is right for you, you have created the foundation to interview well. The clearer you are about "who you are," the more powerful your interviews will be.

Creating Right Livelihood

As I show you the process of interviewing for a new job, I also want to address getting the "right" job for you, which I call Right Livelihood. You can create a job that you love, and you can love the job that you have. I know that may sound like a fantasy, but you can do this. I did it. It was not easy or quick or cheap, but I did it and so can you. Doing so will ease your stress and bring a smile to your face.

When people satisfy a deep need or purpose, they are happy. They create abundance, joy in themselves and others, and excellent products and services. No one ever said you cannot choose a career or profession that makes you happy and satisfies your deepest needs and desires. So what is keeping you from it? I have provided you with a simple exercise in Appendix A to help you clarify your Right Livelihood.

What to Do Before the Interview | 2

The first skill you need to develop is getting the interview. Here are some tools to help you succeed.

Your Resume

Your resume or CV—Curriculum Vita (curriculum: *course*, vita: *life*, meaning *your life course*) has one purpose only and that is to get you an interview. It gives the interviewers enough information to choose to bring you or someone else in for an interview. They also use it to get background information on you so they can formulate questions to dig deeper into areas that interest or concern them. Make sure your resume is written well, as you only get one shot to make that first impression. If, after reading this section, you need more help, there are plenty of books on writing a great resume that you can purchase.

Make sure your resume is rooted in clarity and speaks to your professional background. It should communicate the kinds of things an interviewer wants to know before they spend time with you in person. If, for example, you have five great accomplishments from your last job, include a brief sentence about each of the five, but don't go into minute detail. It will just bore the reader. Tease the reader with tidbits and facts, and then in the interview you can expand and expound on them.

Make sure there are no typographical or grammatical errors! I always recommend that you have your resume proofread by one or two others to ensure that it is error-free and looks professional. Use their feedback to communicate more effectively.

Most recruiters and hiring managers have seen hundreds, if not thousands, of resumes during their careers. These readers have their style preferences but also know exactly what they are looking for when they read your resume. They are looking for experience that clearly characterizes your skills. If your resume does not communicate this information, your chances for getting the interview shrink to zero. The best resumes are clear and concise and answer the questions that the recruiters are looking to have answered.

Many companies use automated database systems to read and store your resume information. To make your resume more compatible with their systems, do not put your name or address in the header or footer. Place your name, address (optional), city and state, phone number, and e-mail address at the top of the page in an easy to read font. I don't recommend that you use an unusual font or a font size smaller than 10 point. I have seen too many resumes that try to be creative, but end up being unreadable.

What questions should your resume address?

Get a piece of paper and pen, and we will create a list of questions that your resume should answer. I will start with the professionals (folks with work experience) and then move on to those who are just getting out of school or have minimal to no experience in the field. So as you go through this exercise, write down the questions that match your situation.

For professionals with experience, ask yourself what are the key traits, skills, personality profiles, and accomplishments someone with your job experience should have. What characteristics make you the best at what you do? If you are not the best, what makes you perform at the level that you do? What have you accomplished in your career that distinguishes you from the competition? What key contacts, experiences, or work products do you have that would capture a reader's attention? What attracts you to this company and why? This could tell you why the company would hire you. Have you worked in high-growth companies? Have you pulled slow-growth companies through tough times? As a professional, consider what this new employer is looking for in filling the role for which you are applying. What do you think the position demands? What questions would you ask someone you were interviewing for that role?

For those with little to no professional work experience, I suggest you have one resume that borrows from an "everything but the kitchen sink" approach and one that is specifically targeted to the job for which you are applying. What have you done in the past that applies to this job? How can your previous success be translated to adding value to the company? Were you in a special program or activity that gave you skills appropriate for this job? See Appendix B for suggested questions.

There are entire books on writing a good resume, so I am not going to go into that here. But you can use these tips as a framework:

- ⊙ Your resume needs to relate to the job you are trying to get.
- ⊙ Make sure your grammar and spelling are correct.
- ⊙ Arrange your employment dates in chronological order (most recent to oldest).
- ⊙ If there is a gap in your work history, give a clear and honest explanation (more on this later in the book).
- ⊙ Do not use abbreviations or acronyms that are indecipherable to the reader.
- ⊙ Do not put your Social Security number on your resume.
- ⊙ Do not put your references on your resume. You can supply them when you are closer to getting the job (more on this later, too).

If you are not clear about what the company is looking for (this is a common occurrence, so don't let it discourage you), create a resume that lists all the things you have done for money and for free (voluntarily). If you are applying for an entry-level job, interviewers won't expect you to have specific experience. However, something you have done may catch their eye, so just throw it all in there. Keep it concise but plentiful.

TIP!

Remember to take that high school diploma off your resume as you move on in your career.

The Internet and your career

Since the late 1990's, the Internet has been a primary tool for recruiters. Therefore, you should set yourself up to take full advantage of this powerful tool. There are many websites that you can post your resume to for maximum exposure. Monster.com, Yahoo.com, and Careerbuilder.com are three of the most popular. Often, there is a recruiting site for your specific field. To find it, do a Google search for organizations that represent people with your skills. These organizations sometimes have a job advertisement or resume posting service. For example, the Society for Human Resource Management in Alexandria, Virginia, provides job listings for HR professionals on their website (www.shrm.org).

Doing searches on the Internet

Aside from posting your resume or searching for jobs, you can and should use the Internet as a research tool. Doing searches on websites such as Yahoo! and Google can bring you a treasure trove of information such as the biographies of the people who are interviewing you, the history of the company or founder, and other information that will give you insight into the organization and help you to impress the interviewers.

The ability to search the Internet will give you great power over the information stored within its ever-expanding websites and data depositories. The best way to conduct a search on the Internet is to use Boolean algebra. Algebra! Yes, it is a form of math, but it is simple to use once you understand it. I have added a clear and concise section on Boolean search techniques in Appendix C.

Making your resume Internet-friendly

Resumes are searched across the web using Boolean algebra. (Mr. Boole invented the form of mathematics we use in computer logic. When people refer to zeros and ones, they are talking about Boolean algebra.) A recruiter enters key words into the search engine in hopes that the most qualified candidates will pop up. Do everything you can to make your resume stand out during these searches. Tailor your resume to include key search terms that would be used when your skills are being sought.

> When I am looking for someone who knows how to design Satellite Power Supplies, I search using the words "Satellite" and "Power Supplies." When I find those words in the body of the resume, I know this is a candidate I will want to investigate further.

Most recruiters will skim your resume to see if particular "buzzwords" (words specific to the job being recruited for) are present. So write sentences using buzzwords (spelled correctly) that are specific to your job function and to each job or educational experience listed on your resume. For example, if you used a particular software package or worked on a project that was notable in your field, include it by name. Do not add buzzwords to your resume in one big paragraph though, as it will appear that you are not focused or directed in your job search. Taking the time to create a readable resume shows the recruiter that you are serious about your job hunt.

Your cover letter

Many people send cover letters along with their resumes. I don't read them because to me they are filled with assertions and contain fewer facts than one's resume. As a recruiter, I am looking for skills that should be represented in your work experience, eliminating the need for a cover letter. If you feel the need to write one or if the employer asks for one, do so.

Your Job Application Form

Most jobs will require you to complete a job application form. This is a standard form, although each company's version will vary in shape and size. Whatever the detail or breadth of the questionnaire, you must fill it out completely and professionally.

There is no mystery to the form. Companies ask you to fill in this form so they have a current record of who you are, where you have worked, where you live, what your past salaries were, who your references are, etc. They use a form to make sure the records for each applicant and future employee are standardized. This is why they ask you to fill out a form that might be redundant to the information on your resume. Companies also use applications to keep track of you for EEOC (US Equal Employment Opportunity Commission) reporting and for possible future employment.

I have seen candidates refuse to fill out the application because they thought they were above it. They are not. Most employers will see this as the act of a jaded person. Companies do not want to fool around with job seekers who think they are better than filling out a simple application.

The information on the application is used to make you a formal offer. It is also used to check your background and confirm your work history. Many companies will have an outside agency do a background or reference check. They will also check with the schools you list as having attended. All schools are required to confirm your graduation date, and your past employers are required to confirm your employment dates.

Do NOT give your Social Security number, driver's license, credit card, or other identification on an application. Your application may be kept in an unsecured file cabinet where those with nefarious intentions could have access and steal your identity. This is not the case in most companies, but there is no reason for them to have that kind of information until you are employed by them. Your Social Security number (and possibly your driver's license) will be needed for payroll purposes and should only be given when you have accepted a written offer for employment.

TIP!

The last thing a company wants to do is fire you for giving false information on your application once you have been hired. Be sure to write accurate and verifiable information on your application and resume.

How to Leave Voice Mail Messages

There is nothing more aggravating than listening to a voice mail message and either not knowing what the caller is saying or having to replay it several times to get all of the information. This happens all the time, and I develop a negative attitude towards a candidate who makes his or her message hard to understand. Here are five simple things to do to leave a great voice mail message every time.

1. Speak clearly, slowly, and with audible volume.
2. At the very least, leave the following: your name, your phone number, and your reason for calling.
3. Leave your phone number in three segments, spacing the area code, then the first three digits of your number, and then the last four digits. This gives the listener plenty of time to write it down.
4. Prepare your voice mail message and leave it on your phone. If you can't understand it, neither will the listener.
5. Type your message beforehand so you have a clear idea of what you are going to say. This eliminates "um's" and "ah's" from your message so you sound confident and concise.

The Recruiter

Companies have internal, contract, or agency recruiters perform the function of finding and hiring new employees. This is a time-consuming and expensive task that companies want done efficiently. The recruiter (or hiring manager) is usually your main point of contact throughout the interview and hiring process.

An internal recruiter works as an employee in the human resources (HR) department of the company that is considering your application. They are knowledgeable about the company's culture, benefits, and work environment. Contract recruiters will be on site at the hiring company but are not full-time employees. They get paid an hourly wage, and though they have an interest in you taking the position, their livelihood does not directly depend on it.

Hiring agencies, on the other hand, are located in a separate office and generally have limited access to the hiring manager, the company culture, and internal staff. There are usually a few agencies working on the same position at the same time. They get paid only if you take the job and stay for sixty to ninety days. If you leave before that time, the agency will likely have to return the fee (20 to 30 percent of your annual salary) or continue to search for candidates to fill the position. When you are applying through an agency, you have more challenges to overcome in being hired, such as greater competition from other candidates.

As I have mentioned before, the recruiter wants you to be "the one." However, this person also serves as the gatekeeper to the hiring staff, making sure the staff's time is not wasted with lesser-quality candidates. They will ask you lots of questions that might put you on the defensive. This can be intimidating and feel like an invasion of your personal privacy.

You should answer all of their (legal) questions and do so in an appropriate manner. The questions I have given you in Appendix E are usually asked by the recruiter. They are designed to qualify your technical and interpersonal skills as well as your interest level (whether you want the job or are just hunting for offers).

Recruiters want to make sure they are getting all of the truth; at times, they can sound like interrogators. Questions like "How much are you earning?" are very private, yet I ask this question all the time. If you don't want to answer right then (you will have to soon), ask the recruiter more questions (see Appendix E) about the job so that you feel comfortable sharing your private information. They are not obligated to keep any information confidential, but the majority of recruiters observe a professional responsibility to keep your information in confidence.

Questions to Ask the Recruiter Before the Interview

Congratulations! You are now at the interview stage of your job search. You have jumped through the first of several hoops on your way to employmentdom.

When recruiters contact you, they ask a ton of questions and give you an opportunity to ask some of your own. I have included a list of questions to ask before your interview (See Appendix E). These questions will help you organize your thoughts and increase your odds of getting the job offer. Take your time asking these questions. Do not pepper the recruiter like an interrogator in a bad police movie. Allow it to be a back and forth dialogue. Remember that you can always call the recruiter again and ask more questions.

What are the job requirements?

Do you know the top reason that people who go on interviews do not get the job? They were not qualified in the first place. I suggest that when you go to the interview, you take responsibility for being qualified for the position. Find out what the job is and make sure you meet the requirements. Trying to sell yourself into a job that you are not qualified for will waste your time. Or worse, you'll get the job only to be fired soon after. Ask the recruiter what skills the employer is looking for and make sure you meet them.

When looking for a job, you may be tempted to take any interview you can. That is a pitfall you will regret. I understand the need to earn a living when bills must be paid, but be aware of how this "not so good" job is going to affect you if you take it. Taking a job that you are not a match for will get you upset and frustrated. Either you will quit or be fired in the near term, or you will be miserable for many years. Don't be afraid to stretch, but consider the ramifications of being clearly unqualified for the

---

I went on an interview for a job that called for me to recruit and hire civilians from age 18 to 80 to be sent into combat as translators in Iraq during Operation Iraqi Freedom. Once the interviewer told me this, I stopped the interview by telling her that I was not the right person for this job. It was apparent to me that I could not waste my precious time, or hers, talking about a job I would not accept in a million years.

A lesson from that job interview was that my recruiter did not give me a clear understanding of what this job entailed. I was only told that I was to hire linguists, as the recruiter had no other information. After the interview, I was upset with this recruiter who had misinformed me about the position. She said she knew nothing about the exact nature of the position and had sent other candidates without hearing this feedback. When a recruiter you don't know sends you on an interview that sounds sketchy, double-check it beforehand so you don't waste your time.

job. Going to the interview or taking the job knowing you are not a match and hoping for a miracle will only cause damage to your reputation and hinder any chance of you working for this company in another capacity.

Also, remember not to hold out for the perfect job that matches all of your needs. You may be able to grow into your dream position once you are established at the company. Many employers will consider a growth path that might take you beyond your expectations. Keeping an open mind about how this job relates to your future could give you more room in picking the "perfect job." Like relationships, there are no perfect jobs, just ones you are committed to making work.

When is the interview?

The best time for an interview is one that works for you. Most interviewers will do their best to arrange a time that works best for you. If you choose a time that puts a strain on your other commitments (child care, current employment, etc.), it is not going to serve you in your interview. Being first or last does not have an effect on your chances of getting an offer.

Here are some questions to ask the recruiter to ensure that you meet the required job skills:
- ⊙ Specifically, what will I be doing on a day-to-day basis?
- ⊙ What technical skills will I need to use in this job?
- ⊙ How many years of professional experience should candidates possess?
- ⊙ Does this job require citizenship or a security clearance?
- ⊙ What do you expect me to produce on a daily basis?
- ⊙ Is it okay that I meet only part of these requirements?

I once brought in a high-level manager to interview. We were to start at 8:00 AM and conclude by 11:00. He did not leave until after 1:30 PM because the initial interview went so well that the hiring staff wanted to move him immediately to the next step of approving his hire by meeting with other managers and senior-level staff. Don't sabotage such opportunities by scheduling yourself too tightly on the day of your interview (if you can possibly avoid it).

Have more than one time slot available in case your first choice is taken. You want to be at your best, so use time to your advantage. If you pick your child up from day care at 5:00 PM, do not make your interview for 3:00 or 4:00 PM. Try not to meet just after lunch, as people are more sluggish. Never meet when you are super hungry or just after eating a big meal. Either situation could affect your ability to concentrate. Keep in mind that the interview may be extended to have you meet more people than originally planned.

How long will the interview take?

Ask the recruiters how much time you will need to allot for specific interviews. Let them know that you are busy but want to spend the maximum time with the interviewers. They should give you a good approximation of how long the interview will last. Always add time to what they say. Interviews can go from 30 minutes to an entire day. To approximate how long your interview will take, you can multiply the number of people you are meeting with by 30 minutes. For example, five people would take you about two and a half hours.

Interviews that are cut short usually mean the interviewers are not interested and don't want to spend more of their time speaking with you. Interviews that appear to go long can be a positive sign that the interviewers are interested in you. But long interviews could also mean other things (that they are struggling to understand your skills, for example). And sometimes the amount of time an interview takes means nothing.

> Recently, I interviewed for a new recruiting position that interested me a lot. I met with two people and it took exactly one hour. When I realized they only spent an hour talking to me, I was impressed that they got to know my skills in a very short time. I left knowing that I would get the job based on the positive signals I experienced from the interview. For me, the signals are feeling excited, energized, and confident. (I did get the job.)

Many recruiters and interviewers like to meet the candidate in a social setting; some do not. Ask if you are going to be sharing a meal so that you can be prepared if you are eating with your interviewers.

With whom will I be meeting?

Finding out with whom you are meeting, including their full titles, will help you prepare for questions. This will also support you in creating an organizational chart. An organizational chart (called an Org Chart by human resources staff) is a document with boxes containing the names and titles of employees.

Many times the recruiter will not be able to tell you with whom you will be interviewing. Don't press them if they don't have an answer, as it is not unusual for the interviewers to change at the last minute due to the uncertainty of people's schedules.

 Often your interviewers get stuck in meetings when they are supposed to be interviewing you. The recruiter or manager will redirect staff to interview you to compensate. Do not be concerned as this is a common event.

What should I bring?

Ask the recruiter what additional information you ought to bring. For example, if you are an artist, you will need to bring your portfolio. You may also be asked to bring extra copies of your resume (which you should bring regardless of what they say), samples of your work product, references, and documentation of your citizenship, education, or previous employment. If you are not sure whether you should bring something, bring it anyway. It is always better to be safe than unemployed. Don't forget the checklist in Appendix F.

Will I need to complete an application?

If you are required to fill out an application (most of the time, you are), have the recruiter send it to you prior to the interview. By getting the application in advance, you can type it out (electronically or with a typewriter) so it looks neat and professional. Most companies require you to complete an application that asks for information you may not know offhand (like your last ten years of employers), so get the form as soon as possible. Bring two signed copies of your completed application with you.

Should I bring references?

I do not recommend that you give the employer references until you are about to accept the job offer. A few hiring agencies or companies may take your references and recruit them for positions they are trying to fill. You may not want your references to be contacted by recruiters who will try and pry them from their current jobs. Tell the recruiter in a polite manner that you wish to provide references when you get closer to an offer in order to protect their privacy. By protecting your references from solicitation, you are presenting a level of professionalism. If the recruiter insists, go ahead and give them. It is rarely the case that a recruiter will call for other reasons aside from checking your background, but it does happen.

Before you give out references, call each of them and make sure it is okay. Tell them who will be calling them, the name of the company, the recruiter, and the position you are applying for so they can be prepared. I have had a small percentage of references come back negatively because the interviewee did not check with them beforehand. The reference checker knows that 99 times out of 100, the reference will come back fine, but don't take the chance of being the 1 in 100.

How do I get there?

Make sure you have accurate directions to the interview location. Recruiters will give you the address and presume you will get directions from the Internet. Candidates take this address and assume the Internet will spit back the perfect directions. Make sure you ask the recruiter or hiring manager for specific directions. Don't be a lone ranger and try to do it on your own. Many companies have odd locations in business parks or complex mini-malls. Getting lost on the way to an interview puts pressure on you and reduces your ability to interview well. It adds stress to an already stressful situation and could make you late.

> Take the time to prepare for your trip beforehand. Make sure you have:
> - ⊙ A full tank of gas
> - ⊙ Several copies of your resume
> - ⊙ Phone numbers to call in case you get lost or stuck in an accident
> - ⊙ Cell phone with charged batteries
> - ⊙ Map and directions
> - ⊙ Something to drink

The best solution is a paper map that gives you details of the streets you will need to take. If you must use the Internet, I suggest www.mapsonus.com, as it is older than most other sites and I find it has the best directions. Drive there beforehand if you are really not sure where it is.

 TIP! Never wing it on the day of the interview. Being late is the most common mistake you could make and the one that will hurt you the most. Being on time is critical, and on time means 15 minutes early.

Will I be tested as part of the interview process?

Ask the recruiter what you may be asked in the interview and prepare yourself. Many jobs require you to take written or oral tests, so be prepared by knowing what is coming.

Will there be a drug test?

Many companies require employees to be tested for illegal drugs. Ask if you will be expected to give a urine, blood, or hair sample. All are used to detect illegal drugs such as cocaine, marijuana, and opiates. If you are using any drugs (prescribed by a physician), let them know beforehand. Regardless of your personal feelings about this policy, employers do have the legal right to conduct such tests.

 TIP! If you eat a poppy seed bagel just prior to the test, it can give a false positive result, so don't eat one for at least two days prior.

How long does the hiring process take and what is involved?

If you want the job, you're going to want to know how long this decision-making process will take. It is very normal to want to know your status in the hiring process. This way, you can plan for your life and prepare your next steps such as giving your current employer two weeks' notice, taking a drug test, planning for a new purchase, or even getting married.

You do have a right to know what to expect next. Find out all the hoops that you will need to jump through when you start talking to the employer, way before you get the job offer. It could take anywhere from one day to several months to get an offer. If the company won't give you an exact date, you can ask the hiring manager or recruiter how long it took them to hire the last employees for this group.

Waiting for feedback on your interview can be the most frustrating part of the process, especially if you truly want the position being offered. Many things can delay your offer, such as people going on vacation, budget adjustments, and the workload of those involved in your hiring process. Expect that your offer will come to you as quickly as the company historically gets them out.

Do Your Homework Before You Go to the Interview

Preparation in life is important, and I cannot emphasize enough the value you will gain by researching and preparing yourself for the interview. Being prepared for your interview will increase your likelihood of getting the job you want. Being prepared in this context brings out your confidence so you are relaxed and at ease during the in-person interview.

Research the company by making an organizational chart

I suggest that you develop an organizational chart before you meet with managers in order to get a thorough understanding of the company and how it works. The Org Chart lays out the management structure of an organization and the relationships between employees. See Appendix G for a blank organizational chart, which you can copy and use to fill in the names of and relationships between the people who interview you.

The Internet is a great place to find all the information you need. Check the company's website first, since it should have the most information about the company in one location. Then start an organized search using websites such as Yahoo! and Google. You can use the step-by-step guide to doing research on the web in

Many years ago, a close friend of mine was applying for an entry-level management position with the United States Postal Service. They said there were thousands (10,000+) of applicants all applying for one position. He had gone through five sets of interviews until his last one, which was with the Regional Postmaster General and a panel of senior executives. To prepare, he researched the organizational chart of the Postal Service.

During the interview, he impressed the panel by identifying the interviewers' relationships to one another, their job functions, and how various groups in the postal service worked together. My friend showed them that he could prepare and be ready for anything. He got the job, and he has been employed with the USPS senior management for the past 15 years.

Appendix C. Your goal is to gather as much information as possible on the people who are going to interview you. A name search could lead you to useful information about them and their company. By doing research, you will impress upon your interviewers that you have good preparation skills and are really interested in their company. I can assure you that if you do even the most basic research, you will have an opportunity to demonstrate your preparedness during the interview. Coming to an interview with this background knowledge will distinguish you from other candidates. For example, if you know that the interviewer won an award in the field, you could ask questions about what he or she did to get it. This will help you create a personal relationship with the interviewer, who will remember your "people skills."

Doing a Google search is easy and can be accomplished with some simple tips. At the search engine's home page, enter the interviewer's name surrounded by quotation marks and hit the enter key. See what comes up and start clicking on the links. If there is too much information to glean anything useful, retype the name with words that are most likely associated with this person, including place of employment, job title, city or state, associations or professional groups he or she may belong to, documents or books he or she has published, or anything else you can think of. For example, if you type in "John Smith" and "Chef," "Cooking," and "Italian Food," all the John Smiths who are involved with cooking Italian food will appear.

TIP!

Make sure you have the correct spelling of the interviewers' names when doing research on the Internet. Often, there are hundreds or thousands of people with the same name. Do as much research as you can, but don't take chances by using incorrect information.

Competitive intelligence

You should know the competitors of your prospective employer, especially if you are already in the field. You may already be working for the competition. Knowing what the world looks like from your interviewers' perspective will give you great insight into what they are looking for from you. It will clue you in to the challenges they face and what goes through their minds when they are trying to distinguish themselves from the competition. If you are breaking into a new field, do not go into the interview without this information, no matter how smart you think you are. Knowing the facts about your future employer's competition is ESSENTIAL.

Key information you should seek out about the competition and your potential employer:
- ⊙ Stock price and trend
- ⊙ Sales over the past five years
- ⊙ Research and development expenditures
- ⊙ Revenue or losses
- ⊙ Recent acquisitions
- ⊙ Recent hiring or firing trends
- ⊙ Contracts recently won
- ⊙ Number of people they are looking to hire
- ⊙ Recent press coverage
- ⊙ Changes in senior level management
- ⊙ Pending lawsuits

Prepare your post-interview thank you notes

It is easy to have a thank you note ready to fill out and mail immediately after an interview. Go to a local stationery store and purchase a set of personalized thank you cards. It may appear like a lot of effort, but it is a touch of sophistication that will distinguish you from the rest of the candidates applying for the same job. You can always use this stationery in your life when sending love notes, thank you cards, or just a friendly hello. I suggest a simple card with your name printed on the front. It does not have to be anything fancy, just neat and professional.

Address and stamp an envelope in advance so that after the interview, you can just write a few short sentences and drop it in the mail (See Chapter 4 for samples).

Dressing for Success

Your appearance leaves an important first impression. Once made, it takes a great deal more time and energy to unmake. Making a first impression that suits your goal is imperative for interview success. The one rule of thumb I suggest for dressing for an interview is to choose clothing that presents you at your best. Your attire should be slightly more professional than the job you are interviewing for requires. What you wear is an opportunity to show that you respect the culture already in place for your profession. Even if the job does not require you to wear a suit, as many do not these days, dressing well for the interview will set you apart.

If you are not sure that you look good, call friends and ask them to see you in your interview attire. Listen to their opinions and make adjustments as needed. Many people come to interviews in a tie that is frayed or in a skirt that does not quite match their blouse. I know this is simple and very obvious, but taking the time to look excellent will increase your confidence and help you get the job.

You do not have to purchase expensive designer outfits, but what you wear should look clean, neat, pressed, job appropriate, and should match. Getting an off-the-rack outfit is fine as long as you take it to a tailor and get it fitted to your body. To make the best impression, the clothes must be altered to fit and accent your best features. If you have put on or lost weight, make sure your suit fits. Don't resist your body shape by avoiding getting your suit tailored after a change in weight.

In short, I suggest that your internal greatness is represented on the outside by your appearance. If you are too casual and informal, you may send a message that you do not take the interview, the company, or the job seriously. If you are too stuffy and constricted in your attire, your interviewer may see you as uptight and restricted. If your clothes are messy and sloppy, they may assume your work will also be sloppy.

Be sure to follow these clothing tips:
- ⊙ Look clean and neat.
- ⊙ Make sure that your hair does not cover your eyes.
- ⊙ Women - do not wear wild hairdos or strong perfume.
- ⊙ Men - get a trim of head and facial hair.
- ⊙ Cover any tattoos and avoid gaudy jewelry.
- ⊙ Limit your jewelry.
- ⊙ The interview is NOT the place to make a statement with your clothing.

So how do you make the best impression? For all office jobs, wear business attire. Business attire is a suit, tie, and jacket for men or a dress, skirt, or pantsuit for women. Dark suits for both men and women connote responsibility and a conservative mindset. A business suit is appropriate for most interviews, even if business casual or casual is the usual attire of the office. If you are a mechanic, you could wear jeans and a T-shirt, but that does not set you apart from others interviewing for the same job. Wear a polo shirt and clean slacks; it might give you the added advantage you need in getting the offer.

If you are an artist, interviewing in a three-piece suit may not make the right kind of impression. You should come in wearing funky or stylish clothes that fit the attire of your peers. Unless you are interviewing for a job where wearing a specific uniform is expected, wear professional attire. If a specific uniform is required, ask the interviewer if you should wear it.

Less than 10 percent of the candidates I have seen don't get it right. Most people tend to dress correctly for their interview. However, I have seen mistakes both in overdressing and underdressing.

Remember that you are looking for a job, not a date. Whether you are a man or a woman, avoid blatantly sexy attire (unless you are interviewing for a Las Vegas casino). Tight, revealing outfits, underwear as outerwear, or suggestive text on clothes are red flags for human resources professionals, who see only the potential for sexual harassment cases and productivity-sucking inter-office romance and gossip. Fingernails should be trimmed to a length that doesn't leave

---

Women

- ⊙ Wear a classic suit or a simple dress with a jacket.
- ⊙ Wear appropriate colors such as navy blue, black, dark green, burgundy, or gray.
- ⊙ Dress in a higher style than the position calls for, but do not overdress.
- ⊙ Avoid wearing clothes that are tight, revealing, or too trendy. It may be the very latest fashion, but it will not impress the interviewer.

Men

- ⊙ Wear a suit or sport jacket with trousers that match.
- ⊙ Choose neutral colors. Dark blue, black, or gray work best, but greens and tans work too.
- ⊙ Wear a tie even if you will never wear one once you get the job.
- ⊙ Pick shoes that are leather, and that are cleaned and polished.
- ⊙ Match the color of your socks to your shoes.
- ⊙ Make sure your fingernails are trimmed and clean.

---

an observer wondering how you keep from stabbing yourself. The polish should be closer to a color your mom might wear than to a color that your kid sister would choose.

Having facial hair as a man will not hinder you most of the time, but in some fields it gives your prospective employer the sense that you're unreliable. If your peers wear beards or mustaches, then feel free to wear one yourself. If you wear a beard or mustache, make sure it is trimmed and looks neat. Trim any hairs you may have in your ears or nose. Those can be very distracting to an interviewer.

The bottom line is that you must choose and prepare your interview outfit in the days before the interview itself. Do not leave it to that morning to discover you don't have any shirts pressed or your last pair of stockings has a run or your favorite tie has a stain. Save yourself unwanted extra stress on the morning of the interview by having your complete outfit, including all accessories, checked out and laid out the night before.

> Recently, I interviewed a woman who had drenched herself in a perfume I found awful. As she walked down the hall, she left a trail that made the managers and me notice (and not in a good way). She did not get the job because of her skills (or lack thereof), but I can assure you the heavy perfume did not help her case.

Prepare Yourself Mentally

While getting your physical appearance in excellent shape is an important part of a successful interview, it is even more important to get yourself prepared mentally and emotionally. Your mindset during the interview is the most critical component in delivering a stellar interview and getting the job.

Visualization Exercise

Find a piece of paper right now…I'm waiting…if
you don't have one at hand, use one of the blanks
in the back of this book. Write down the following:
"(YOUR NAME) is the (YOUR NEW TITLE)
of (YOUR NEW COMPANY NAME)." For
example, mine might say, "Lorne Epstein is the
new Chief of Surgery at Coney Island Hospital."
Write this down 50 times on a sheet of paper, make
copies, and tape them to places that are highly
visible for you. Write this sentence any way you
want (crayons, markers, vertical, diagonal, block
letters, cursive); the most important thing is that
you see it. Make it colorful and have fun with it.
Make it attractive so that you are drawn to look at
it and read it. Your brain is very easy to program
and will create what it truly believes.

To prepare yourself mentally for the interview, clear your mind
and imagine getting the offer. Imagine the amount of money you
will be paid and what the letter looks like. See yourself happy and
excited now that you have landed this job. See yourself in your new
office doing the job you wish to do. Add to and embellish this story
until it becomes an absolute truth in your mind. The story you
tell your mind is powerful. This practice will help your body act in
alignment with your mind during your interview.

The Night Before the Interview

Remember that the time you spend to prepare your body and mind
for the interview will pay off when the interview actually occurs.
Therefore, spend the night before your interview setting yourself
up to win by being at your best. Prepare your clothes and make
sure your directions, resume, ancillary materials, pen, stamped and
pre-addressed thank you cards, and application are ready to take in

a briefcase or folder. Also put in some breath mints and a lint roller for that last-minute spruce up.

The night before the interview, make sure you get plenty of sleep. When you awake, take time to be good to yourself. Eat a good breakfast and take a relaxing shower. If you have a sensitive stomach, do not eat prior to your interview. Drink plenty of water and keep your food intake to what feels comfortable. It is best to fuel your body so your energy does not fade during the interview. If you have nothing more than a cup of coffee or a soda before your interview, you may be jittery and lacking in focus and/or energy.

Good Luck!

Listen

to

You're Hired Radio!

Lorne's podcast can be heard at iTunes.com

"You're Hired Radio" with Lorne Epstein entertains and informs you on issues relating to your Job and Career. Lorne shows you how to get a raise, how to interview, and how to get the job of your dreams. He covers issues from the perspectives of the employee and employer.

What to Do During the Interview | 3

The Interview Context

The purpose of your resume is to get the interview. The purpose of the interview is to get the job. That's right; you get the interview so you can get the job. It could be a phone interview or in person, but either way you will need to have some conversation with the recruiter or hiring manager before you get a job offer.

Of course, you are not the only one "selling yourself" during an interview. The recruiter or hiring manager is also selling you on the position. The interview is your opportunity to better understand what makes this position the right one for you.

Your interviewers want to hire you. Remember, that is the big secret. They want to meet you and know that you are the person they want. Knowing this going into the interview should put you at ease. They have already decided to hire the perfect candidate. There are only two questions you should be considering in the interview process. One is, Are you the perfect candidate for this job? The other is, Does this job meet your needs? That is it. Do your best to answer these two questions and you will have accomplished a great deal. Getting the job or not is moot if you are not a fit for the employer or if they are not a fit for you. If both answers to these questions are yes, then you can tip the scale by applying these simple, but highly effective, principles outlined in this book.

The trick to interviewing is to distinguish yourself from all the other candidates the interviewers will see. Many times, candidates who interview for a job are at about the same caliber as one another. So you want to take every opportunity to present yourself as the most professional, organized, and well-equipped person for the job. That is the heart of the matter—making sure you have honed every skill at your disposal.

Be on Time

Being on time for an interview means getting there 15 minutes before your scheduled appointment. Being on time for your interview (or anything in life, for that matter) is more than just getting there early. It is a method we use to communicate about what is important to us. If you are generally late in your life, I invite you to look into why that is. Don't stop with the first thing that comes to mind. Look a little deeper and see what you are communicating to others when you are late.

> In case you do not see what being late means, listen to these direct quotations from hiring managers:
> ⊙ "Being late is the kiss of death to an interview."
> ⊙ "The later you are, the more you are communicating that you are not responsible and can't be counted on."

If you are going to be late, call the recruiter or interviewer as soon as possible. Make sure you have the phone number of the receptionist, recruiter, or hiring manager to call in case of an emergency. People understand that delays can occur and most will give you some slack. But if you don't call and are late, you will hurt your chances of getting the job.

Arriving 15 minutes before your interview is scheduled will give you enough time to settle yourself, go to the restroom, get a drink of water, or just sit and read your notes about the company. There is nothing like settling in once you have arrived. Being early gives you greater confidence than rushing into an interview without any time to acclimate yourself to the new environment.

Being too early sends an incorrect message. Showing up too early (more than 15 minutes) makes you seem too eager. And if you come to the job interview too early, you may inconvenience, and perhaps annoy, the interview team. They are usually busy and may have several candidates in at the same time. The recruiters will have to stop what they are doing to take care of you. Be respectful of their time. If you arrive more than 20 minutes early, wait in the parking lot, a coffee shop, or some place nearby.

> I had a young man fly in from out of town the day prior to his interview. We had flown him in from Illinois and put him up at a local hotel. The day prior to his interview, he called me and left a message asking when he should arrive at our location. I called his hotel room back and left a message saying 9:00 AM. The next morning he arrived at 7:00 AM, tired and wasted from his travels. I felt bad for him as he was setting himself up to wreck his day-long interview. I asked if he had gotten the message and he said no, but he had seen the blinking light on the phone in his hotel room. This was poor planning on his part and had the potential to negatively affect his interview. He was made an offer, but partially because I made sure no one knew about his mistake.

Be Mentally Prepared

The most important thing you can do with your extra 15 minutes is to get your mind and attitude ready for what is about to happen. Come to the interview with the expectation that you will get an offer, that they will be professional, that the interviewer will ask you relevant questions, and that you will be clear and articulate.

Relaxation Technique
If you find yourself breathing hard and your heart is racing, here is a simple relaxation technique that takes one or two minutes. Take a deep breath and do not stop until you have reached the count of ten. Take plenty of time to bring your breath in.

Hold this breath and count to seven. Then slowly release the air, counting down from ten to one and making sure you finish breathing out by the time you reach one. Do this several times and your entire body will relax automatically.

I was interviewed at a place I had sent my resume to several weeks before. I was expecting it would be disseminated and read by those who would be interviewing me. When I got there, the second question they asked me was "Do you have a copy of your resume?" I thought they were very unprofessional and made my mind up on the spot that I would not take an offer from them. I have learned since that this happens a lot more often than I thought. So I make sure to keep extra copies with me to avoid getting caught short. As a recruiter, I always send a copy of the resume to the interviewing managers well in advance. But it never fails; managers either don't read their e-mail or just don't have the right copy on hand, leaving it up to the candidate or me to deliver one promptly.

Visualization Technique

Before you go for the interview, take a few minutes to get your mind in the proper state. Close your eyes and imagine what it would be like working at this company. See yourself being happy and excited about this new job possibility, in the role you want, earning the money you want, having the kind of impact you want. Hold these thoughts as your personal truth. If thoughts of doubt come up, that is okay. Just go back to the thoughts of you getting the job. Do this for five minutes or until you are feeling confident that this job is yours.

Bring Copies of Your Resume

It is easy to presume that the people you interview with will have a copy of your resume. You sent it to them. You assume they read it. So why do you need to bring extra copies? The people you interview with are busy and may forget to have a copy with them, or maybe the recruiter never got them a copy, or sometimes they just don't take the time to read it until the last moment. If this happens, having your resume in hand will prevent delays and will show that you are prepared to get the job done. Have a copy of your resume for each person you are set to see. If you're not sure, bring five copies so you are covered. This is the easiest thing to do to show your interviewer that you are responsible and prepared for the unexpected.

 E-mail yourself your resume so that you have a copy available at all times.

Sell Yourself

Many candidates forget that the purpose of the interview is to sell your best assets to the client – period. The word "sell" has become taboo in our society. This is a false notion that needs to be changed now. We are always selling who we are. If you are married, you sold yourself to your partner. He or she bought who you are and keeps buying it every day. That means you are the one doing the selling. It is a subtle sell and it works for you. Take that ability and use it in your interview.

Your job is to share, clearly and honestly, your work experience and to highlight stories that exemplify what you are capable of doing. If you excel at relating to people, let them know that in the form of a story. Tell it as a narrative with details and make sure your story works. Tell it to a friend a few times to see what they think.

On the following page is an example of a concise story about my skills. What do you notice when you read it? What information does it tell you? If you have issues with talking positively about yourself, get over it! No, really, get over it. It is time for you to

Sample Narrative:
I started working as a recruiter eight years ago, and during that time I have hired over 200 highly skilled engineers, software developers, and managers with too many skills to recall. You would hire me to source, screen, and hire highly qualified employees quickly. I am qualified to do full life-cycle recruiting from sourcing candidates to negotiating offers and checking references. I am flexible and can work both in teams and on my own. I prefer to have as much control in the hiring process as possible. My current and past employers are available to give you great references on my past performance.

take charge of your future and practice selling yourself to others. Join Toastmasters, take a speech class at a local community college, and practice in a mirror or with a friend.

Be Clear About What They REALLY Want From You

Knowing the expectations of the manager will have a beneficial effect on how you interview. There are critical questions you must ask before you leave the interview regarding the specifics of the job for which you are applying.

Expectations of your performance can vary from company to company, even if you have the same job title. Make sure you know the expectations your manager has of you. The answers to these questions could affect your future raises or promotions.

Find out if you are expected to go out for beer on Friday afternoons or join sports teams in order to fit in. Your work has a culture and you will need to adopt it if you expect to grow there.

Leave your interview knowing what you are expected to do and what results you are expected to generate. Get this in writing if you can; sometimes it can come in the form of a job description. However, some companies won't provide one, so don't press the issue if they do not.

I have taken jobs where they expected me to do things I would have preferred not to do, like mopping the floors or cleaning the toilets (really). I took a job once not knowing how much I would be paid or with what frequency. This became a bone of contention between the employer and me, so much so that I eventually quit. I did not feel that they cared about my needs, which is very important for me. Had I gotten this in writing beforehand, my expectations would have matched my results, thereby reducing my frustration and upset. I am sure I would have been more patient with the schedule of salary payment had I known it in advance.

The key here is that you are creating a new relationship with expectations for both yourself and your employer. Knowing what is required of you before you start will help you in deciding whether to take the job or not. Take charge of your life and be responsible for knowing what you want and what is expected of you in return.

Raise Your Hand and Ask Questions

One thing that displays your intelligence is your ability to analyze data and ask relevant questions. Don't be afraid to ask questions. It will take you down the path to more questions, revealing more about the job for which you are interviewing. Having questions for later will help with your follow-up calls. It gives you a stronger reason to call back and shows you are thinking about what was said to you.

Creating a list of questions

Create a list of at least six questions to ask the interviewers. You can have a list of twenty or more but have a handful that you can count on. Writing down twenty questions will give you at least six good ones to ask. You could easily forget questions, as your head will be filled with a ton of new information, so having them written down will assure that you ask them. Always have something to say when they ask if you have any questions. Not asking questions won't hurt you, but remember you are looking to be smarter than the average bear. See Appendix H for a list of questions.

They Asked You WHAT?!?! What You Cannot Be Asked in an Interview

There are rules about what an interviewer can ask you. They were created to protect your privacy and eliminate biases in hiring practices. There was a time not long ago when companies would qualify candidates on factors unrelated to the job, such as marital status, personal lifestyle, or religious affiliation. Laws now regulate what can and cannot be asked.

Here is a list of things that you cannot be asked about in an interview.:

- Anything about your marital status or family obligations.
- Your use of drugs (legal or illegal) or alcohol *(however, they can give you a drug screen)*.
- The number of workdays that you missed due to illness. *(You can be asked: "How would you rate your overall attendance record?") NOTE:* This subject has become even more sensitive with the passage of the Americans with Disabilities Act.
- The number of workers' compensation injuries you have had or claims you have filed.
- If you are a smoker or non-smoker. *(An interviewer can let you know that you will be working in a "smoke-free" facility.)*
- Your arrest record *(A criminal background check may be done which will turn up any convictions you have had.)*
- Your religion, beliefs in God, or spiritual affiliations.
- Your race or national origin.

- Your age, height, or weight.
- Your disabilities, unless they will interfere with your work. In that case, they may have to provide you with tools to mitigate any limitations if they are within reason.

If you are asked these questions, you can politely remind the interviewer that the question is inappropriate or you can just say you would rather not answer. I encourage you to report inappropriate questions to your state's department of labor. If they are not responsive, you can contact the Department of Labor in Washington, DC (www.dol.gov).

If you have reservations about a question, there is only one safe policy: Don't answer. Ask the interviewers the purpose of the question and why they are asking. If you still do not want to answer, politely tell them you do not believe the question is relevant to the position.

Samples of inappropriate questions

The following are questions that can be viewed as an attempt at gaining illegal information. Your response should be: "I would rather not answer your question." Once you have said that or something like it, you may want to excuse yourself and end the interview. Remind yourself that working for a company that would ask these types of questions is not for you.

- Do you have a distinctive accent? Are you Asian?
- Flagstaff has a rather small Jewish community; from the sound of your name, that might be of interest to you. *(Attempt to gain religious information)*
- This department is made up entirely of men. As a female, would you find that difficult? *(May imply that gender is a qualification)*

- Is your spouse looking for work in this area?
  (Attempt to gain marital status information)
- Do your children attend school? How old are they?
- Could we help you get in touch with a minister, rabbi, etc. while you are visiting our campus?
  (Attempt to gain religious information)
- Are you a minority? *(Not job related and is illegal.)*
- From your credentials, we were expecting someone much older. How old are you?
  (May cause applicant to question whether age is a factor in the decision. Age discrimination is illegal.)

Questions you can be asked in an interview

Demonstrate what you know. This could be in the form of a hypothetical simulation or technical questions you will need to answer:

- What are your strengths?
- What are your weaknesses?
- Describe a past success and how you made it happen.
- Describe a past failure and what you learned from it.
- Why are you leaving your current position?
- Describe your work history and explain why you left your past jobs.

Who the Heck Did I Just Talk To?

When you make your follow-up calls, make sure you address people by their proper names and titles. This is where the organizational chart in Appendix G will come in handy. Before, during, and after your interview, write down the names of the people you just spoke with. When you leave the interview, you should fill out the organizational chart. This will take care of remembering who is who and where they belong in the company relative to everyone else.

Notes are Not Just for Passing

Taking notes will help you remember what was said in the interview and will give you a place to write down questions to ask later. However, don't get too buried with your pen and paper, and make sure to stay focused on the interviewer. Always ask if it is okay to take notes while you are in the interview. Some people prefer that you don't write things down while they are talking to you, so respect their request if that is the case.

Saying I and Not WE

When you are asked questions about the work you performed, make sure you answer in the first person, starting your sentences with "I." Many candidates answer questions using "We" and not "Me." This never works. It tells the interviewer you're either not listening or you did not do what you are saying you did. If you answer, "We designed that advertising program," the interviewer will think that you worked on a team and supported the process in some way. They will not get a clear understanding of your abilities. To avert this error, practice answering questions in the first person using "I" and me." Take a few minutes and have a friend ask you questions about the work you do in a mock interview. Have them repeat back to you what they heard you say. Listen to what they say—is it what you meant to communicate?

Breaking Bread

Sharing a meal with your future coworkers can be your moment to shine. You have an opportunity to conduct yourself in a very comfortable setting. The interviewers will have their guard down and will tend to be relaxed. If they are not enjoying themselves, be cautious about working at this place. Most people allow themselves to be real when they are out of the work environment, such as when they are eating a meal. Either way, you will see the social side of your colleagues.

If you are funny, take this moment to share some humor. If you are knowledgeable in history or some new technology, share this. Don't hesitate to talk shop; it will give you the chance to show your passion for work.

The meal will leave an impression of what kind of person you will be to work with. This is as important to you as it is to them. You don't want to work some place where you will always be an outsider because of your personality type. For example, if the group is composed of very gregarious people, you may feel uncomfortable if you have a more reserved personality.

Cash, Moolah, Dinero, Shekels, Rupees, and Greenbacks

Yes, it is true, do not talk about money until they bring it up or an offer is being discussed. Chances are, they will ask you what you want to get paid. There are two schools of thought on this. One is to tell them what you want, and the other is to see what they offer. The latter may get you more money depending on the employment market and your worth to them. The response you give is situational and depends on what you know about the market rate for your skills.

If you choose not to reveal information about what you want to get paid, you can reply, "What does this position pay?" and let the recruiter answer. He or she may not give you a direct answer, to which you can respond, "What is the average salary in your company for someone like me?" Talking about salary in these general terms will help you get an idea of what you will be paid.

When you talk about money, remember that it is easier to negotiate down than up, so start with a salary higher than you want.

Usually, there is little room for negotiation for most positions in most companies. The reasons are numerous, but the major one is that large and medium companies have compensation structures designed to keep new hires in line with current staff. Making sure everyone gets paid the appropriate salary is a top priority for human resources professionals.

If you are looking for a specific amount of money and need to be sure they can meet your figure, ask the recruiter or manager in advance. You can say, "I am earning $80,000 a year now. Can this job exceed that amount?" It is okay to ask up front if this position can support your salary needs. Do not ignore the issue. Many people leave the question so far off the table that they are shocked when they see their actual offer.

Candidates who make an issue of the offer tend to turn managers off. I have seen candidates not get a job because they asked for too much or kept asking for more after their first request was honored. Hiring managers are happy when you accept their first offer. You can help them by making sure their first offer is one that you will accept.

Wrapping Things Up

The following sections will help you end the interview and assure that you have covered all of the important topics.

Check it out!

When you are in the interview process, do not forget to notice the work place. Does it look neat and tidy or is it a mess? Do they have equipment and tools that you will need to do your job? If the office equipment (computers, copiers, phones, etc.) does not appear to fit the organization (too old or in disrepair), ask why and if new ones are coming. Many organizations will spend little on tools and expect their employees to provide them. One of my employers did not have the test equipment needed to allow the engineers to do their work. The engineers had to borrow or bring in their own testing tools to get their job done. In some cases, employees brought in their own screwdrivers. Ask questions about what kind of resources are available. Their answers will tell you about the company's ability to grow, support, and nurture their work force. If there are virtually unlimited resources, you can bet they will invest in you.

Tell them about it! Sharing all of your juice

Do not forget to tell the interviewer about your skills and what you are bringing to the position. Be your own best interviewer and make a list of your top skills that are relevant for this job. Put them on your note pad so you can recall them in an instant. Leaving an interview not having said all that you wanted to can happen, so don't worry about it. You can always call back, but remember that most of what sticks in the interviewer's mind is what you tell them in person.

If you've got plans, let them know

Tell the interviewer about any impending vacations or major life plans that will interfere with your work schedule. Things like going to night school or taking a vacation are important for the employer to know up front. Once you are hired, they will have an unspoken expectation that you are available to work at the hours agreed to and maybe more.

Letting them know up front makes it much easier to take the vacation, leave work early for classes, or whatever you plan on doing. Your employer won't mind and will understand that you have a life and have made arrangements before taking this job. But surprising them later on will only get in your way.

Do you want this job or not?

You may presume that your interviewer knows you want the job because you're interviewing for it, but that is not enough. Once you are sure you want the job, let them know. Forgetting to tell the interviewer that you want the position could cost you the job. Your desire and enthusiasm to work with this company is taken into consideration. Employers want to hire people who show a desire to work for them. Being apathetic, uncaring, and nonchalant about the position will communicate your disinterest and allow another candidate who is more outwardly excited to get the job. Once you are in the interview process, let them know what you like about the company and that you would accept a reasonable offer. Conversely, let them know right away if you are not interested.

Lay the groundwork for follow up

Before you leave the interview, ask the recruiter and hiring manager if you can call to follow up. Most interviewers are willing to speak to you later, but it is important that you be considerate of their time. Making follow-up calls will give you a chance to ask more questions, mention any information you neglected to say in the interview, and keep you on their minds.

Sayonara!

When you have completed with the formal part of your interview, make sure you can answer these questions:

1. Do I want this job as I understand it?
2. If not, what would have to be different so that I would want to take it?
3. Do I have my interviewers' names, titles, and phone numbers so I can follow up and create a personalized organizational chart?
4. Have I seen enough of the facility and spoken to all the necessary people?

If you have clear answers to these questions, you have done your job well.

How to "Be" in an Interview

So far, we have talked about the nuts and bolts of interviewing—how to research the employer, how to prepare for the interview, what questions you should ask and shouldn't answer. All that stuff is important, and the more you follow these guidelines, the better your interviews will go. However, in the end what gets you the job—or not—is not how well you "do" the interview, but how you present yourself to your interviewers. Ultimately, they will make their decision, in large part, based on how they feel about who you were "being" in the interview.

If you are not familiar with this term, your being is the essence of how you show up to others. It is not how you feel or think or what you know. It is always occurring in the core of who you are. Being is simple to see in others but sometimes harder to see in ourselves.

To put it in other terms, your "beingness" is the way that other people experience you and your personality. Examples of ways of being include open, powerful, confident, joyful, sad, disinterested, or angry, just to name a few. It will serve you in all areas of your life to distinguish the way you are being. You can then adjust the way you're being to learn to generate the results that you desire in your life.

The following sections address some of the ways of being that are particularly helpful in getting the job that you want.

Be confident

When you arrive for your interview feeling confident and assured that you are the best candidate for the position, you will interview well and give the non-verbal message that you are the best candidate for the job. Being confident can be tapped into using several techniques, such as being prepared and having your homework done. Another is to prepare your mind-set. What you believe in your core is what will usually occur. If you know without a doubt that you will be hired for this position, you will show up as confident. Before you embark on your interview, ask yourself how confident you are about doing your best and getting this job. If you are 100 percent sure that it is yours, great! If you are less than 100 percent sure, what is in your way? What stands between where you are right now and being confident that the job is yours? Do not confuse nervousness (which is a natural and helpful feeling) with doubt.

If you have researched the background of the company and position, prepared a list of questions, presented a good physical image, gotten a good night's sleep, and arrived with time to spare, you know you've set yourself up to win. So relax and have fun with your interview.

Be related to your interviewers

It is important that you create a rapport with the interviewers. It is tricky to give tips on this since it is about how you are being rather than what you are doing. Maybe that says it all, but let's see if I can uncover what this means for you.

When you meet your interviewers, connect with them like an old friend. Make them feel comfortable. You may be thinking that is their job. But take it from one who has been on both sides of the interview table, sometimes the interviewer has more at stake and experiences more anxiety about the interview than you do. They may be unsure about their interviewing skills or they may be under a lot of pressure to fill an opening right away.

So take care of your interviewers. Do everything you can to put them at ease. After you answer a question, allow them to speak or to sit in silence and collect their thoughts. Be honest and friendly and responsive to the unspoken cues they may be sending you. This is a skill that you will get better at as you interview more often.

Be authentic

I always appreciate authenticity. Being authentic means allowing your true self to show through. If you don't have a good answer to a question, say so. The interviewer will appreciate knowing what your limits are. Your interviewer will know that you are who you say you are because your words will match up with the experience they are having of you.

An interview is not the place to try the old adage, "Fake it 'til you make it." So if you realize during the interview that you don't have the required qualifications, say so. If you are nervous, say so. If you need to use the restroom or get a drink of water, say so.

If you are excited about the job and really want it, blurting out "hire me!" may or may not work. Saying something like "I really enjoyed the interview and would accept a reasonable offer for this position" would probably be a better way to go. Being authentic does not mean blurting out what's on your mind. Being appropriate and effective is the route to go.

The Truth, the Whole Truth, and Nothing But the Truth

Now, while being authentic and open and honest are all good ways of being, there can also be the problem of "too much of a good thing." That is, while you want to be real and connected and share yourself with your interviewers, this does not mean you should let it all hang out. Remember to keep your honesty and openness on a professional level.

The sections that follow will outline a few things to look out for in terms of being honest and authentic in your interview.

Acting appropriately

Your personality is important to how people experience you in the world. You can't change it, so don't even bother trying, especially if it works for you and creates the results you want.

However, if your personality style is perceived by other people as outrageous, confrontational, opinionated, or controversial, you may need to rein it in somewhat during your interview. Some things that may seem funny or serve as a great conversation starter with your buddies over drinks will come across as obnoxious and inappropriate in an interview.

> Here are some tips to follow:
> - Never make jokes about sex, politics, religion, race, money, or any other topic that has a charge to it.
> - Only ask questions of the interviewer that they could or would ask of you.
> - Never insult the interviewer or people who work in the office.
> - Be polite and on your best behavior.

Create appropriate behavior by reviewing what you plan to say before it leaves your mouth. Practice with yourself or a friend.

When you start working there, you can tell jokes. Remember, the farmer won't buy the cow if you give the milk for free. (See how inappropriate my humor was?)

Avoid getting too friendly or casual with the people you meet, unless the interviewer encourages it. If they lead you in a conversation that is more relaxed and you feel comfortable going there, don't be concerned—it is now apparent that the interview is going to be more relaxed and casual.

Blabbermouth – Telling too much of the truth

Those of us who want to be honest sometimes get ourselves into trouble. I have been like that—there are times when I just say way too much. I have seen this occur with candidates that I have interviewed as well. The point of this story is that you don't want to raise unnecessary doubts about extraneous issues that are not relevant to the position or that wouldn't otherwise come up with your references or background check. In an interview, it is not always appropriate to go into the "whole truth" of any situation.

Liar, liar, pants on fire – Not telling the truth

This leads me to the "Truth." The "Truth" is a funny thing as there is rarely an absolute "Truth" that we can all agree on. Even gravity changes from place to place on Earth. When sharing the "Truth" about our work history with our interviewers, we tend to embellish the facts with color, which is a healthy component in selling our abilities.

However, lying or hiding a critical fact can come back to haunt you. If a lie comes back to bite you, it will have a more deleterious effect on your job than coming clean up front. If you were fired from your last job, do not hide it. The way you could say such a thing is, "I was let go from my previous position because…" and you will have taken the bite out of the issue. It is for you to calculate the risk involved in not sharing every little detail of your life. Some companies do a more thorough background check than others, but if they find out that you lied, it will be hasta la vista, baby.

Large companies tend to do a more extensive background check, which includes reference checks, salary confirmation, and educational experiences. During the checks, the recruiter or human resources generalists will ask your references to characterize your working and personal skills. Anything that happened could come up in this check.

How to Clarify Issues in Past Work Experiences

Everyone creates some negative experiences during his or her career. This is nothing to be ashamed of. If you feel a negative experience will come out, then share it up front, clearly explaining what happened, how you handled it, what you learned from the experience, and how you will handle a similar situation in the future.

I am going to show you how to create a true and explainable story of your professional past. Many people are fired for cause, meaning they did something so incorrect that they were let go. This should not and will not end your career.

Some of the issues you may need to cover are presented here with some recommended responses. Don't use these responses unless they are true for you; they are intended to be a guide to coming up with a respectable explanation for aspects of your work history.

You could not afford to live on the salary you accepted

It is okay to tell your interviewer that you took a job because you needed the money to pay your bills. It is not uncommon, given the last few years of economic trends, that you could not find a

I recently interviewed a guy who was amazing in his field as a test engineer. He was technically a match and just the kind of person we wanted to hire. He was asked to share about a job he had three years ago, and he told us that he was fired. My hiring manager made a presumption that he may have stolen company property. He jumped on this and would not allow himself to see the truth. The truth was that the candidate had not stolen anything. I asked the manager to be open to hiring this person, but it was no use. His mind was made up and nothing I did would change that. I called all of the candidate's references and did my own version of Columbo to check the facts. I found nothing negative, but had to tell the candidate we were not going to make him an offer. Had he not shared this piece of information, he would have been hired.

job in your field. Millions of workers accepted lower-level positions and took a pay cut.

You were accused of stealing from your past employer

This is a serious accusation and can lead to criminal charges. If you have been arrested and convicted of this crime, tell your interviewers. Always presume they will do a criminal background check because most companies do. To explain this issue, you must dig deep into whatever possessed you to commit a crime and be ready to share that. Whatever the reason, you want to acknowledge the character flaw, take responsibility for it, and tell them what concrete actions you have done to better yourself, such as drug treatment or counseling.

You did not meet your employer's expectations

This is an easy one to mitigate. You can share with your interviewers that the job and your skills were not a match. Explaining it in detail will show your interviewers that you know your skills, limits, and potential. We all have limits and everyone has weaknesses that can be a challenge to overcome. The point of your explanation is to show that you have learned from your mistakes and that you want to find a job that is a better fit for your skills and abilities.

You were not challenged by your work

Many jobs are structured below our ability; when you tell your interviewers that, you are again distinguishing your strengths and capabilities. Interviewers like to hear that you know what roles you fit best, based on your personality, behavioral styles, likes, dislikes, and other variables.

Your employer treated you unfairly

It is not uncommon for employers to treat their employees unfairly. If that was your case, you need to clarify things, but only if it is going to come up in the reference check. Clarify your situation by sharing what happened and how you dealt with it in a responsible manner. Some companies will hire you based on reference checks from some past employers and not others. You have the right to tell them whom they can and cannot call for references. However, if you don't allow them to contact any of your past employers, you will be sending up a red flag that could hinder your offer.

You were harassed

If you were harassed and charges were filed or some type of record exists, you can choose to share this or not. The hiring manager's perception, at best, is that you are a poor victim of a really bad crime. At worst, they will think that the same could occur at this new place of employment. Do you want either perception to be in his or her mind? I don't think so. Be mindful of how they will contextualize what you are saying.

You were accused of harassing/assaulting someone

This is a tough one and must be addressed, again, if you know for a fact that they will find out. If you were prosecuted, regardless of your true innocence, you must nip this in the bud as you move forward in your interview process. Like all the other points I have talked about here, timing is important. You do not need to share this information in your first interview or possibly at all.

In conclusion, dealing with a checkered past is no fun, but at times it is necessary. Do not avoid it if you feel it will hinder your chances of getting the job you want. A lot of people have sordid pasts and manage to make it anyway. Sharing your past in a responsible manner, and as a learning experience, will demonstrate your ability to turn adversity into opportunity.

What to Do After the Interview | 4

Pray! Just kidding. (Or am I?)

Send Thank You Notes IMMEDIATELY

As soon as you leave the interview, take your pre-addressed, pre-stamped thank you notes and write a quick letter to all the key individuals you met. Key individuals are those people who decide whether you get an offer or not.

What to write in your thank you note

Keep it simple, short, and to the point. If you want the job, tell them so and give them one or two reasons why. You can also make a comment about the interview; don't hesitate to be creative if the mood strikes you. If they made you a verbal offer, then you can use this time to tell them you are strongly considering it or that you want to give your formal acceptance once you receive an offer in writing. Use the letter to make the impression that you care, that you're interested, and that you are thoughtful in your job search. But keep your communication to one or two key points.

Here are some examples of a letter you could write.

Dear Recruiter,

Your team's credentials and the high level of work they produce impressed me. I would be honored to accept a position with your company. As I mentioned to you in the interview, I am very busy at my current job, and I would need some time to complete my projects there. I would be available to start three weeks from the date I receive an offer letter.

Thank you,
Mary Candidate

Dear Hiring Manager,

My experience in electrical engineering and your group's reputation in that field are what initially attracted me to interview with your team. I was even more impressed after meeting you and your team. I have several questions and will be giving you a call in the next few days for clarification.

I would be interested in considering a reasonable offer to work with SoftTech. I will be graduating on May 15th and will be available to start three weeks later on June 7th. Thank you for inviting me in for an interview. I enjoyed meeting you and hope we are able to work together soon.

Sincerely,
Lorne Epstein

Dear Mr. Manager,

I enjoyed meeting with you, Sally, and Bob today. I found the group to be very professional and forward thinking, particularly regarding the direction to develop the Internet as a source for revenue. I am very interested in the position and would accept an offer that was commensurate with my experience and education. I look forward to speaking with you soon. I can be reached at 999-345-9999.

Sincerely Yours,
Lorne Epstein

Mail it

Once you drop the notes in a nearby mailbox, you are done. The interviewers should get them within a day or two, which will impress the heck out of them. Everyone likes to get a handwritten note that does not have "Invoice" at the top. Your interviewers will be left with a positive feeling after reading your brief letter.

E-mail vs. handwritten note

E-mail is a good supplement to a handwritten note, but I don't suggest it as the way to make the most positive impression. A handwritten note from you on a nice piece of notepaper is the best way to follow up. Using e-mail to follow up and ask more questions is totally appropriate and will help when trying to contact busy people.

Write Down Your Impressions

After you send your thank you notes, sit in your car or at the bus stop and write down your thoughts and ideas. Take as long as you want. Record your thoughts and feelings about how you did, frustrations about things you said that you thought were silly, and anything else that comes to mind. Write down what you noticed about the place and the feel of the interview.

While working at a defense company, I was asked to hire an IT specialist with expertise in finance. I recruited a lovely woman whose technical skills were a great match for the job. She came in for an interview and was very excited about the position. The hiring manager was a stodgy man who would always drag his feet after interviewing someone. He was not going to hire this woman unless something drastic happened. The woman called me frequently, and I recognized that she would be an excellent fit for this group and the company. So I took the lead and instructed her to write a short thank you note to the hiring manager telling him she was interested in the position. Several days later, the manager came storming into my office holding her letter and gushing about how this was the candidate to hire. Thanks to that letter, we hired her, and when she started, the manager was very positive towards her.

This will help you hone your interview skills so you will do better the next time you have an interview.

Now the Interview Is Really Over, so Take a Deep Breath and Relax

The interview process is draining no matter who you are. I have done it more than most, and it still puts a dent in my energy level. So reward yourself for your hard work; I always play some upbeat music, loosen my tie, and get some fun food.

Some of us (not me, of course – smirk) have a tendency to beat ourselves up for not doing a good job. Just remember that interviewing is a tough endeavor and that you did the best you could. If you could have done better, you would have. You are a bright and talented individual who just went through a process during which you were judged in a critical, albeit professional, manner.

Your opinion of how you did and how you looked is important. However, if you are already highly self-critical, then maybe you are not the best person to ask how the interview went. However you performed in the interview, know that a professional interviewer can separate your nervousness from your skills and talents. And you can always call or write to add more information later.

Follow Up

When you last spoke to your interviewers, you created a game plan for yourself as to when and how you should follow up. When you "follow up," it shows that you are interested and want the job. Through this process, you can learn more about how you interviewed and what steps to take next. You can also add or make corrections to the interviewers' perceptions of you. And you will find out if you are still being considered for the position.

A phone call is best, but you may only be able to reach them by e-mail. Do not be a pest. Plan your call for a time you know will be convenient for the recruiter or hiring manager. Recruiters work during the day for the most part, so call them during their work hours. Be available for their calls during their work hours as well, including lunch time, if need be. Most managers and recruiters don't like to stay late to work.

As I said in the previous chapter, you should have agreed to a time and process for contacting your interviewers during the interview, so be sure to stick to your agreements. You are helping your chances for success if you follow up with them when you say you will.

First, get outside feedback

Feedback is a process by which you hear what others see you

During one interview, I was just a mess. I had on a shirt that was too tight around my neck, and it made my tie look awful. I never put my contact lenses in and left the house with my glasses on, which made it a bit harder to see. I had forgotten to bring my research or copies of my resume with me, and I was nervous as all get out. When I spoke to the interviewers, I gushed and said goofy things. I interviewed with two people for only 30 minutes each, which I feared was too short. In the end, though, I got the job offer. What mattered was that I had done research and was able to quote their previous sales figures, which impressed them. They had copies of my resume and did not need the ones I did not bring. I was nervous, but I still answered their questions and I gave them a clear description of exactly how I would do what they were hiring me to do.

saying, doing, or being. It enables you to experience how others experience you, a task that is impossible for you to do on your own. Getting feedback will support your life as you see what you look like from outside yourself. Seeing yourself this way is the best way to learn, grow, and become the next greatest version of who you are.

Therefore, before making your follow-up contact, talk through the interview with a friend, colleague, parent, or whomever to get feedback on how you did. This can be as easy as just venting your experience to a good buddy until there is nothing left to say. Your friend can hear your tone and the feelings behind your words. Then ask them these kinds of questions: How do you think I did? Did it sound like they were interested in me? What do you think I could do next to improve my chances of getting the job? Was there anything in what I said that I should be concerned about?

Use the feedback process to find holes in your understanding of the job or the company, or to discover some negative impression you may have made inadvertently. Then make sure to address those issues in your subsequent contact with the interviewers.

What to say in your follow-up call

Before you call, remember that you are setting up an opportunity to ask questions and share more information about yourself. Prepare for the call by writing down questions (see Appendix I) and information you want to share. Planning will help you get the information you want while leaving the best possible impression.

Telling them you are or are not interested in the job is a good place to start. Most companies prefer to make you an offer only if they know that you are interested in taking the job. So if you are very interested, say so.

Conversely, if you know the job isn't right for you, let them know. It is professional, shows consideration of their needs, and leaves the door open for future possibilities with that company. One example of how to turn down an offer is to say, "I really appreciated your time and feel that I have other opportunities to pursue. Can I keep your company open as an option in my future?"

Ask all the questions you did not ask in the interview or small things like what is the pay schedule. Make sure that when you get the offer, you are fully informed so you can make a clear decision. You can review Appendix I for a list of suggested questions to ask.

Have Patience

Be patient while you wait for an offer or rejection. This can be challenging when you are desperate or very hot for this job. If you are unemployed, I suggest you follow up this interview with more job searching. You will capitalize on the success you gleaned from this interview by getting another interview. Do what you can to mitigate the anxiety you might be feeling by using some of the techniques here:

1. Land more job leads and interviews.
2. Conduct research on your list of potential interviews.
3. Exercise more often and take long walks.
4. Have lunch with friends.
5. Create informational interviews.
6. Network at professional group meetings.

Have as many irons in the fire as possible. The more work you do to create a large pool of interviews, the less you will worry about getting one particular job.

Getting the Offer

The recruiter or hiring manager will usually call and make a verbal offer. When this person calls, have a pen and paper ready to write down all the details. You want to take good notes so you can compare this offer with others or with your current employment. The offer may be conditional, based on the completion of a drug test or reference check.

Expect to receive an offer letter with the details of the offer, including salary, stock options, vacation, and benefits summary. Only when you get an offer in writing is it considered a real offer.

Therefore, no matter how enthusiastic someone sounds on the phone, DO NOT take any action before receiving a written offer letter. NEVER quit your current job, terminate your lease, or buy new work clothes without a written offer. Companies do, on occasion, rescind offers, and you have no recourse if all you have is a verbal offer (go to page 73 for more information on rescinded offers).

Timeline for the Offer

Never accept the offer without thinking about it for a while, but make sure the company knows how long it will take you to make the decision. There is great temptation to take the job right away, especially if you have been out of work for months. You should feel free to consider an offer for up to a week or more. Taking the time to reflect can help prevent you from experiencing "buyer's remorse" once you accept this new challenge in your life. Even if you think you will say yes to the offer, you may find out something that you did not know about by taking a day or a week to decide. You may want to get more information before you accept their offer, so be sure to ask all the questions you have.

Be clear on the time frame for making your decision

Ask how long you have to make this important decision. Most recruiters will give you plenty of time, but some may press you for a quick answer. Ask the recruiter beforehand if there is a rush and how much time you can take to make your decision. If you need more time, ask for it then.

Be responsible for your experience of this part of the process. Many people come to this point and feel rushed, cajoled, pressured (that is my favorite one), or just plain disregarded.

The recruiter's job is to hire you as quickly as possible, so keep that in mind when he or she is working hard to move the process along. I have heard candidates say many things to give themselves a little more time, including that they are considering other jobs, need to talk with their spouses, or simply that they need time to consider the offer. A company may view you as more professional for reviewing the offer. However, your actions can influence your manager's feelings about you in a pejorative way if you hesitate and take more time than allotted.

Once you have agreed upon a decision timetable, NEVER keep them waiting beyond your deadline. They may decide to rescind your offer and make it to another candidate. Remember, they need you now. The sooner you start, the happier they will be.

Communication Strategy

Keep the recruiter or hiring manager informed of your search

Once, I brought a candidate in from out of town to interview with the hiring managers. He wanted to move to the area for his family. He liked us, and we liked him. After the interview, I asked him if he would accept an offer. He said no for reasons that were irrational to us. Several months later, he called me up saying he wanted the job. I told my managers, but now they were hesitant and skeptical of this candidate's intentions. Also, since we had interviewed him, more local candidates with the skills we were looking for had become available. Our group was about to spend $65,000 to relocate him and his family, and there was a concern that he would leave once we got him down here. This would never have been an issue had the candidate been clearer on his decision to take the job in the first place. Some opportunities are not available the second time around.

and what you are thinking of doing. This is so important and here is why. You will choose one company to work for, and once you get there, your forthrightness and honesty will gain you trust from the start. The companies you say no to become irrelevant. Managers and recruiters know that you could be interviewing with other companies, but unless you tell them otherwise, they could presume that you are accepting their offer.

Keep your word when you say you are going to do something on a certain day. If things change (and they always do), call and renegotiate to a later date that you WILL keep.

If you choose to take the job, don't be wishy-washy about it. Take it, fill out the forms, and follow their hiring procedures fully and wholeheartedly.

TIP!

One factor to consider when making your decision is the benefits package that's offered. Read the material carefully, no matter what. You may have a benefit you never use because you didn't know it was available.

Getting a Counter Offer

A counter offer happens when your current employer hears that you are leaving and offers you a promotion, more money, or some other benefit to keep you working for them. I have seen many employees take the counter offer only to regret it later.

In case you are tempted to accept a counter offer, here are twelve good reasons not to:

1. What kind of company do you work for where you have to resign before they pay you a fair wage?
2. The money for the counter offer is likely coming from your next raise. Most companies have strict wage and salary guidelines that must be followed. In giving you this money, they are usually breaking policy.
3. Once you accept the counter offer, your employer may start looking for your replacement, one whom they can pay a lower salary.
4. Your employer is now aware that you are unhappy. Your loyalty will always be in question, and you will now be out of the confidence of management.

5. When you are due for your annual review, your employer will remember that you were looking and could hold your lack of loyalty against you.

6. If business slows down, you could be the first one to be laid off.

7. Your reasons for not wanting to stay with your current employer will still be troubling you, regardless of your acceptance of this counter offer.

8. Statistics show that if you accept a counter offer, the probability is extremely high of either voluntarily leaving in six months or being let go within one year. National figures indicate that 89 percent of people accepting counter offers are gone in six months.

9. Accepting a counter offer is an insult to your intelligence and a blow to your personal pride because you know that you were bought. It is up to you to accept the insult or not. If you accept, then your employer's regard for you will immediately decline. The fact that you can be bought will preclude the possibility of your employer regarding you as an equal.

10. Once the word gets out, the relationship that you now enjoy with your co-workers will never be the same. You will lose peer group acceptance and will forever be that person who

Here are a few questions to ponder when you are considering the counter offer:

⊙ If accepting a counter offer is like acknowledging infidelity, will it be forgiven and can it be forgotten?

⊙ Will your career track remain blocked if you accept it?

⊙ Will your responsibilities be expanded?

⊙ Will you have to report to a person you don't respect?

⊙ Most employers don't like being fired, so are they temporarily buying you to later dispose of you on their terms?

⊙ Is this a ploy to avoid a short-term inconvenience by your employer?

⊙ What are your realistic chances for promotions now that you have considered leaving?

was bought back for more money than they are making. The acceptance of your peers will diminish in subtle ways at first, but the trend will continue. The group will become more cohesive without you. Eventually, the group will exclude you from the support structure. Groups can be quite predictable in these situations.

11. Once you hand in the written resignation letter and then allow your boss to talk you out of it, they will feel you can't make a decision and stick to it. They may feel you were using the other offer as a ploy to get attention or money.

12. Just don't do it.

The irony of considering a counter offer is that you rarely gain anything. Take the new job. If it doesn't work out, you may still be able to go back to your old employer with respect and say you made a mistake. In the meantime, you have the advantage of getting into a new and exciting career opportunity.

Responding to the Offer

In making your decision, you have three options:
1. To reject the offer.
2. To accept the offer as given.
3. To accept the offer if certain conditions are met by the employer.

Rejecting the offer

You may have many reasons for rejecting the offer. If you are clear that you do not want this job no matter what is offered, call the company and let them know. You can hurt your reputation and future prospects for being hired if you drag this process out when you know you don't want the job. Making it clear that you are rejecting the offer as soon as possible is very professional.

Accepting the offer as given

When you are sure you are going to accept the offer, follow the directions and get the offer letter signed and back to the employer as soon as possible. You may need to take a drug test or go through an orientation process, so the more time you give them to get you processed, the sooner you will start working. Make sure you make a copy of the letter for your records if one is not included.

Asking for more money

I get more questions about this than anything else. It is not too hard to know how much you are worth to most employers because most folks get paid within a market range. This market range is a salary that most people holding that job get paid. There are some fluctuations based on factors such as geographic location, strength and size of the company, their current financial situation, and more.

For example, in most parts of the country, an electrical engineer coming out of college with a bachelor's degree would have gotten paid around $30,000 in the mid-1990's. From the late 90's until 2001, they could expect up to $70,000 because of the high growth in technology. As of 2004, they could expect $40,000 or a little more. During this time, salaries of existing engineers went up about 20-30 percent (if they changed jobs), causing the current decline in salaries for engineers just coming out of school.

Sometimes, higher salaries can be deceptive. They often come with longer work weeks, arduous travel, or challenging work conditions. Many attorneys who are recent graduates must work up to or more than 100 hours per week to garner salaries above $100,000, while a local district attorney will be paid half as much for working 40 hours per week.

You should want to get paid the most that an employer can reasonably pay you. Take these basic factors into account when determining your worth in dollars and cents:

1. Your education, training, and certifications.
2. Your technical skills.
3. The number of years of experience you have in this field.
4. What your peers within the hiring company earn.
5. How hard it is to find someone like you in the marketplace.

The only way to negotiate a higher salary than your peers is to illuminate all of your skills during the interview process. This could include, but is not limited to, knowledge of a particular piece of software, awards you've won, contacts you have at other companies, patents you hold, papers you've written, or books you've published. Speaking a foreign language or having lived in another country could offer the employer the ability to expand into that country, so that could be a valuable attribute to mention. If you can present yourself as a complete solution to a particular business problem the employer is having, you can set yourself up to ask for more money.

Asking for more benefits

Often, companies cannot give a higher salary than what was originally offered. This is because they do not want to create salary inequities. Salary inequities occur when a new employee at the company is paid a higher salary than someone who has similar credentials and responsibilities, but who has been with the company longer.

Instead, you can ask for more benefits. Some benefits you can request include extra days of vacation or perks normally saved for their best employees. Asking for perks or other benefits allows the company to increase the value of the deal while keeping your salary in alignment with that of your peers.

Sign-on bonuses

Sign-on bonuses became the buzzword in the 1990's when unemployment was down and companies had to pay extra for good talent. Sign-on bonuses are given to keep you happy while at the same time keeping your salary in alignment with your peers. You do not want to be the highest paid person in your group if you don't have the most experience. It will make you a lightning rod for a future layoff.

Sign-on bonuses have value, but not as much as you may think. Since they are paid in one lump sum, usually in your first paycheck, they are taxed at the highest possible rate. This could cut your payment by 35 percent or more. So a $10,000 bonus turns into a $6,500 payment. Remember this when asking for one.

If the Offer is Rescinded

I have seen candidates get great offers with the promise of a new job and more money, only to have their hopes dashed when the company takes back the offer. There are no two ways about it: this is a real bummer. In many cases, you have legal rights and could be compensated if this happens to you. If you have quit your current job, relocated, or incurred other expenses and have an offer letter in hand, you may have a case. There is a body of law under personal injury tort called detrimental reliance. In layman's terms, detrimental reliance means that your belief in or reliance on the contract (which has been broken) resulted in a loss or detriment of some kind. If you choose this option, be sure to get yourself a good labor or employment attorney.

Why companies rescind offers

You may have thought that once you get an offer in writing, there is no chance of the job falling through. Unfortunately, that's not the case. While it doesn't happen frequently, even written job offers are sometimes rescinded. Three reasons why this might happen include:
1. External factors outside the control of the person doing the hiring.
2. Problems encountered with your drug test, reference and background check, or security clearance.

3. Something about your post-offer conduct that gives the company "cold feet" about hiring you.

There are external factors that will stop an offer. For example, a company-wide hiring freeze may have been imposed between the time of the offer and the time of your response. Or the company was suddenly acquired, and your department is being eliminated altogether. Usually these things don't happen out of the blue, so if you've done your research properly (like I discussed in the beginning of the book), you should be able to anticipate this possibility.

There is little that you or the person who wants to hire you can do about these situations. Your only options are to:
1. Accept the situation and look for another job.
2. Wait and work through the problem in hopes of getting the job.
3. Negotiate some kind of financial settlement (see an attorney).

If you lose a job offer because you failed a condition of your employment, such as testing positive on a drug test, there is usually little you can do. The same is true for passing your background and reference checks. This is why I urge you to address any blemishes from your work history during the interview. Admitting to and explaining any skeletons that might be found during a background check is much better for you than having your offer rescinded.

Your employer could experience "cold feet" for an infinite number of reasons. One reason could be your behavior once they make you the offer. That's why it's so important to project a positive image even after you've received an offer. Raising issues that should have been covered during the interview process or demonstrating dissatisfaction with aspects of the job may cause the employer to rethink the decision to offer you the position.

TIP! I'll say it again—NEVER quit your job or incur other financial expenses or obligations unless you have an official offer letter in hand.

The following is a sample of a real letter from an attorney to an unspecified human resources department on how to rescind an offer.

ATTORNEY LETTER ON HOW TO RESCIND AN OFFER

Your offer can be rescinded. When you do, tell her by phone (taking note of the day and time) and confirm it in writing. You can say that it is obvious from her questions when considering the offer that the work hours don't fit with her personal needs, and as a consequence, you are rescinding the offer. Since she has not accepted, it should not be a problem.

It could be a problem if she has quit her previous job or has moved because of your offer. She could then claim damages under the personal injury tort of detrimental reliance. So tell her ASAP. Since she has not accepted yet, she should not have given notice at her other place of employment.

The above situation is why you should include language in your offer letter that says the candidate should accept by signing the offer letter and faxing you a copy.

Conclusion | 5

Interviewing can be a difficult, challenging, and time-consuming activity that is filled with frustration and disappointment. Yet it is a process that most of us will engage in several times over the course of our lives.

I hope that this book helps you get a job that you love and create a career that is satisfying. For all of your effort, you should experience the joy, freedom, and abundance that a career designed for you can provide.

If this book has been useful, let's keep in touch. Please write and tell me how your job search or your career is going. I will post updates and resources on my website that will support you in your interviewing and job searching process. I also do workshops and speaking engagements, so look for me in a town near you (check the website for my speaking calendar).

I hope that you read this book a few times, use it as a reference, and buy copies for friends to use. If you find that you become experienced in interviewing, I invite you to help others in seeking a job that brings them satisfaction and joy.

Contact me at:
Lorne@YoureHiredBook.com
www.YoureHiredBook.com

Listen to "You're Hired Radio" on iTunes.com.

Listen

to

You're Hired Radio!

Lorne's podcast can be heard at iTunes.com

"You're Hired Radio" with Lorne Epstein entertains and informs you on issues relating to your Job and Career. Lorne shows you how to get a raise, how to interview, and how to get the job of your dreams. He covers issues from the perspectives of the employee and employer.

There are tons of books and people out there that will support you in getting a job, but I have a few tips of my own to share with you as a bonus to my guide to interviewing.

Right Livelihood is work that supports your life and is "right" for you. Right Livelihood makes you happy, allows you to be fully expressed, and earns you an income that you enjoy.

Give yourself several hours to complete the following exercise. To do a thorough job, you must apply your focus, creativity, and flexibility. Like all good things in life, this takes work. If you don't like to work alone, get a friend or a group of friends to do this exercise with you. Having friends work with you will help you generate more ideas to create the job of your dreams.

Before you start this exercise, ask yourself the following questions and listen to what the voice inside you says. Be honest: you don't have to share your answers with anyone else.

- What makes me happy?
- What do I enjoy doing? (work-related or not)
- If I could do anything regardless of time, money, or education, what would it be?
- What would I need to do for that to occur?
- What is stopping me?
- What would I do if my goals were to:

Earn Enough Money	Make a Difference
Be Happy	Have Fun
Have Satisfaction	Learn New Things
Be Appreciated	Travel
Be Valued	See New Things
Be Accepted	Be Challenged
Be Effective	Experience Life Fully
Work with a Purpose	Live a Vision

I invite you to take this opportunity to create the job you truly desire.

What you will need for this three-phase exercise:
1. 50 sheets of paper.
2. Pen or pencil.
3. Friends to help you brainstorm.

Phase One

1. What does my soul tell me to be doing? This seems like an abstract question, but it's not. Ask yourself this question if you are not clear and listen. Listen for the voice in your head that speaks back to you. This question asks if your avocation (what you love to do) is in alignment with your profession (what you get paid to do). Everyone who works must ask this critical question at some point in life. What is your passion for this job?
2. Outline on paper what matters to you most in life. This is not job-related—just a free flow of thoughts and ideas about the things that excite and inspire you. Be creative and fun. Let your thoughts flow to paper and do not erase anything you write. This exercise is meant to give you an abstract, high-level view of your priorities. It is okay to leave out details and write what matters to you most. It could be saving the world, feeding the hungry, creating peace on the planet, becoming a millionaire, being a mother or father, helping children, meditating, or teaching others. Keep it all there and don't erase a thing.
3. When you are done, read your outline and then repeat the process. Allow your brain to drain all its thoughts. Don't take anything out—just keep adding ideas. When you can't think of anything else to write, this part is complete.
4. Once you think you have finished, put your outline down and let it sit for a few days or a week—however long you

wish. The idea is to allow your brain to start percolating ideas that you will use in Phase Two.

Phase Two

1. On a sheet of paper, write down all the things you like to do. This could be reading, running, playing or watching sports, watching TV, writing, cooking, getting or giving a massage, planning, helping others, dancing, paying bills, or keeping organized. Make a list of things you do that you enjoy. Once you think you are done, read it over a few times and add more thoughts as they come.

2. Using a separate sheet of paper for each thing you like to do, write down that one thing at the top of the page. For example, you might write "planning" on one sheet, "cooking" on another, "shopping" on still another, and so on.

3. Taking each page one at a time, write down at least twenty (or more) ways that people earn a living doing that task or activity. For example, if you have "writing" for one, you could put author, journalist, copywriter, speechwriter, and editor. If you wrote down that you enjoy speaking, your list might include radio personality, TV host, minister, salesperson, teacher, stadium announcer, and public relations. Move on to the next page until you have completed a list for each task or activity.

4. Find ten jobs you didn't know existed and add them to each list above. You can ask your family, friends, or co-workers for suggestions.

5. Now you have a very large list of jobs to choose from. There is no rhyme or reason for picking one over another, other than the choice you make about what your Right Livelihood is.

6. Now it's time to narrow your choices. Be creative. Eliminate those jobs you are less interested in doing. Keep those that get you excited. Pair jobs up or create a mixture of three,

four, or more that suit you. For example, if traveling and writing are two of your favorite things to do, you can be a travel writer. What similarities do you notice among the things that you like?

7. Create a top ten list on a new sheet. These jobs can read any way you like. For example, "Underwater diver, writing for *National Geographic* only six months out of the year." Look at your list of ten and put a line through two of your least favorites.

8. It's time to stop Phase Two and take a break.

Congratulations! You've done a lot of work moving towards your Right Livelihood. Take at least a day or more to let the work you have done take root in your mind.

Phase Three

1. Now it's time to take another look at your list of favorite jobs. Put a line through your two least favorites. Repeat this until you are left with only two choices.

2. Once you have your top two choices, circle the one that makes you feel happier.

3. You have now identified a possible Right Livelihood. Write it at the top of a blank piece of paper. Also write down all the things you like about this job and what makes you happiest about it.

4. Find someone who has this job now and set up an informational interview. An informational interview is a conversation with a professional about the work he or she does. Your objective is to find out what it took to get that job. Ask this person questions such as:
   • What is it like to have this job?
   • What education or skills does one need to be hired for this position?

- What has the job market been like during your career?
- What can I expect to get paid during my career?

5. If you still want that job, make a list of all the things you have to do to get it. Do you need more education or training? Do you need new connections or to develop a skill?

6. Declare a date by which you will have this job. Write this date down on a piece of paper and put it in a prominent place in your home, like on the refrigerator.

7. I suggest you get a coach or someone you can be accountable to in creating this new job. Hire one or ask a friend to help you create a list of things you need to do and a timeline for completing them. Then ask them to help you stay on track so that by the date you say you will have this new career, you do.

Congratulations! I wish you all the best in creating your new Right Livelihood.

Get the job and live your dream!

Questions Your Resume Should Answer

For Professionals

1. What specific hard (technical) and soft (interpersonal) skills do you have that meet the position's requirements?
2. What makes you the best at what you do?
3. What makes you perform at the level you do?
4. What have you accomplished in your career that distinguishes you?
5. What key contacts or experiences do you possess?
6. What notable work have you done in your past?
7. What about your previous employers makes you an attractive candidate and why?
8. What have you accomplished in your avocational life that distinguishes you?
9. What measurable metrics did you achieve or help others to achieve?
10. What special projects were you involved with and how did they help the organization?
11. What would you expect to read in someone's resume who was applying for the same position?

For Non-professionals

1. What volunteer activities have you done?
2. What work experience do you have that fits the job?
3. What have you done well?
4. What does this job require of you?
5. What do you know about the industry?
6. What is the organization's history?
7. How can your previous success translate into adding value for the prospective employer?
8. Were you in a special program or activity that gave you skills that will be useful in this new role?

Boolean Searching on the Internet

A Primer in Boolean Logic

The Internet is a vast computer database. As such, its contents must be searched according to the rules of computer database searching. Much database searching is based on the principles of Boolean logic. Boolean logic refers to the logical relationship among search terms, and is named for the British-born, Irish mathematician George Boole.

On Internet search engines, the options for constructing logical relationships among search terms extend beyond the traditional practice of Boolean searching.

Boolean logic consists of three logical operators:
- OR
- AND
- NOT

Each operator can be visually described by using Venn diagrams, as shown below.

OR

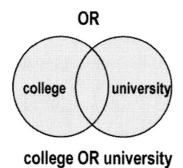

college OR university

Query: I would like information about college.

- In this search, we will retrieve records in which AT LEAST ONE of the search terms is present. We are searching on the terms **college** and also **university** since documents containing either of these words might be relevant.
- This is illustrated by:
  - the shaded circle with the word college representing all the records that contain the word "college"
  - the shaded circle with the word university representing all the records that contain the word "university"
  - the shaded overlap area representing all the records that contain both "college" and "university"

OR logic is most commonly used to search for synonymous terms or concepts.

Here is an example of how OR logic works:

Search terms	Results
College	17,320,770
University	33,685,205
college OR university	33,702,660

OR logic collates the results to retrieve all the unique records containing one term, the other, or both.

The more terms or concepts we combine in a search with OR logic, the more records we will retrieve.

For example:

Search terms	Results
College	17,320,770
University	33,685,205
college OR university	33,702,660
college OR university OR campus	33,703,082

AND

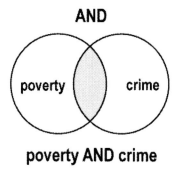

poverty AND crime

Query: I'm interested in the relationship between poverty and crime.

- In this search, we retrieve records in which BOTH of the search terms are present
- This is illustrated by the shaded area overlapping the two circles representing all the records that contain both the word "poverty" and the word "crime"
- Notice how we do not retrieve any records with only "poverty" or only "crime"

Here is an example of how AND logic works:

Search terms	Results
Poverty	783,447
Crime	2,962,165
poverty AND crime	1,677

The more terms or concepts we combine in a search with AND logic, the fewer records we will retrieve.

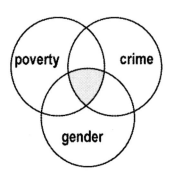

For example:

Search terms	Results
Poverty	783,447
Crime	2,962,165
poverty AND crime	1,677
poverty AND crime AND gender	76

A few Internet search engines make use of the proximity operator NEAR. A proximity operator determines the closeness of terms within the text of a source document. NEAR is a restrictive AND. The closeness of the search terms is determined by the particular search engine. Google defaults to proximity searching by default.

NOT

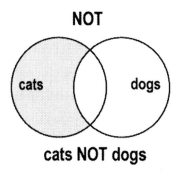

cats NOT dogs

Query: I want information about cats, but I want to avoid anything about dogs.

- In this search, we retrieve records in which ONLY ONE of the terms is present
- This is illustrated by the shaded area with the word **cats** representing all the records containing the word "cats"
- No records are retrieved in which the word "dogs" appears, even if the word "cats" appears there too

Here is an example of how NOT logic works:

Search terms	Results
Cats	3,651,252
Dogs	4,556,515
cats NOT dogs	81,497

NOT logic excludes records from your search results. Be careful when you use NOT: the term you do want may be present in an important way in documents that also contain the word you wish to avoid.

Boolean Searching on the Internet

When you use an Internet search engine, the use of Boolean logic may be manifested in three distinct ways:

1. Full Boolean logic with the use of the logical operators
2. Implied Boolean logic with keyword searching
3. Predetermined language in a user fill-in template

Full Boolean logic with the use of the logical operators

Many search engines offer the option to do full Boolean searching requiring the use of the Boolean logical operators.

Examples:

    Query: I need information about cats.
        Boolean logic: OR
        Search: cats OR felines

    Query: I'm interested in dyslexia in adults.
        Boolean logic: AND
        Search: dyslexia AND adults

    Query: I'm interested in radiation, but not nuclear radiation.
        Boolean logic: NOT
        Search: radiation NOT nuclear

    Query: I want to learn about cat behavior.
        Boolean logic: OR, AND
        Search: (cats OR felines) AND behavior

Note: Use of parentheses in this search is known as forcing the order of processing. In this case, we surround the OR words with parentheses so that the search engine will process the two related terms first. Next, the search engine will combine this result with the last part of the search that involves the second concept. Using this method, we are assured that the semantically-related OR terms are kept together as a logical unit.

Implied Boolean logic with keyword searching

Keyword searching refers to a search type in which you enter terms representing the concepts you wish to retrieve. Boolean operators are not used.

Implied Boolean logic refers to a search in which symbols are used to represent Boolean logical operators. In this type of search on the Internet, the absence of a symbol is also significant, as the space between keywords defaults to either OR logic or AND logic. Many popular search engines traditionally defaulted to OR logic, but as a rule are moving away from the practice and defaulting to AND.

Implied Boolean logic has become so common in Web searching that it may be considered a de facto standard.

Examples:

    Query: I need information about cats.
        Boolean logic: OR
        Search: cats   felines

This example holds true for the search engines that interpret the space between keywords as the Boolean OR. To find out which logic the engine is using as the default, consult the help files at the site. Nowadays, there are few engines that use OR logic as the default.

    Query: I'm interested in dyslexia in adults.
        Boolean logic: AND
        Search: +dyslexia   +adults

    Query: I'm interested in radiation, but not nuclear radiation.
        Boolean logic: NOT
        Search: radiation   -nuclear

Query: I want to learn about cat behavior.
Boolean logic: OR, AND
Search: cats   felines   +behavior

Predetermined language in a user fill-in template

Some search engines offer a search template which allows the user to choose the Boolean operator from a menu. Usually the logical operator is expressed with substitute language rather than with the operator itself.

Examples:

Query: I need information about cats.
Boolean logic: OR
Search: Any of these words/Can contain the words/Should contain the words

Query: I'm interested in dyslexia in adults.
Boolean logic: AND
Search: All of these words/Must contain the words

Query: I'm interested in radiation, but not nuclear radiation.
Boolean logic: NOT
Search: Must not contain the words/Should not contain the words

Query: I want to learn about cat behavior.
Boolean logic: OR, AND
Search: Combine options as above if the template allows multiple search statements

Quick Comparison Chart: Full Boolean vs. Implied Boolean vs. Templates			
	Full Boolean	**Implied Boolean**	**Template Terminology**
OR	college or university	college university *see note below*	any of these words can contain the words should contain the words
AND	poverty and crime	+poverty +crime	all of these words must contain the words
NOT	cats not dogs	cats -dogs	must not contain the words should not contain the words
NEAR, etc.	cats near dogs	N/A	Near

* This search statement will resolve to AND logic at search engines that use AND as the default. Nowadays most search engines default to AND. Always play it safe, however, and consult the Help files at each site to find out which logic is the default.

Where to Search: A Selected List	
Feature	**Search Engine**
Boolean operators	AllTheWeb Advanced Search | Dogpile | HotBot | Ixquick | ProFusion
Full Boolean logic with parentheses, e.g., *behavior and (cats or felines)*	Ixquick | MSN Search Advanced Search
Implied Boolean +/-	Most search engines offer this option
Boolean logic using search form terminology	AllTheWeb Advanced Search | AltaVista More Precision Google Advanced Search | Lycos Advanced Search | MSN Search Advanced Search
Proximity operators	Google [by default] | Ixquick

This appendix used with permission from Laura B. Cohen from her website: http://library.albany.edu/internet/boolean.html

Questions a Recruiter Will Ask Prior to the Interview

1. What kind of job do you want to get?
2. When can you start?
3. Why do you want to leave your current job?
4. What about this job interests you most?
5. Are you still working?
6. What is your current salary?
7. What compensation are you seeking?
8. Tell me about your experience with____.
9. How long have you been doing _____?
10. What did you do at your last company?
11. What kind of work environment do you prefer? (casual, professional, eclectic)
12. When can you come in for an interview?
13. Are you interviewing with other companies? (It is a good idea to answer this honestly.)
14. Are you a United States citizen?
15. Is there anything in your background that would prohibit you from getting a security clearance?
16. Are you willing to relocate?
17. Are you willing to travel? If so, how much as a percentage of your work month?

1. What does this job entail?
2. Do you work for the company?
3. What can you tell me about the company?
4. Why are you looking for someone to fill this position? (growth, last person quit or was fired)
5. What kind of growth is the company experiencing?
6. Is it a casual or professional work environment?
7. What kind of person are you seeking?
8. What kind of technical skills are you seeking?
9. What kind of personality traits do you think best fit this job?
10. How long have you been looking for someone to fill this position?
11. Are you currently interviewing other candidates for this position?
12. (If yes to 11) Where in the interview process are you?
13. With whom would I be interviewing?
14. Could you explain the company's organizational structure?
15. Who would be my boss, who is his boss, etc?
16. What are the goals of the company?
17. What are the goals of this group/division?
18. What projects is the organization working on?
19. How many hours per week do you want someone to work?
20. Is there travel involved?
21. Does this job require a security clearance, or will I get one down the road?
22. What is the pay range you are offering?
23. How often do employees get paid?
24. What is the history for employees getting raises and promotions?
25. How many years of experience are you seeking? Are you flexible?
26. Is it okay if I only meet part of these requirements?
27. How will personality factor into getting this job?

28. Is there any training available to employees?
29. Is there tuition reimbursement?
30. What is the annual turnover rate? (This is the percentage of people who leave the company each year. This number will tell you how well the employees like the company relative to other companies in the same industry.)
31. How many employees do you currently have? (This will tell you how well their business is doing. Ask yourself if you believe that they are on the upswing and growing or downsizing.)
32. What is the volume of business you plan to do this year? (Never ask about prior years, as you should know this from your research.)
33. What should I be prepared for, going forward?
34. What could stand in the way of my getting a job offer?

Pre-interview

Research the company ☐

Research the company's competitors ☐

Prepare organizational chart ☐

Get directions to the interview location ☐

Ensure appropriate attire ☐

Bring the following tools:
    Proofread resumes ☐

    References ☐

    Completed application ☐

    Pen and pad ☐

    Addressed and stamped thank you cards ☐

    Breath mints ☐

    Lint brush to clean clothing ☐

    Something to drink ☐

Post-interview

Grade facility:
      Cleanliness

      Support staff

      Equipment

      Work space

      Proximity to home

      Proximity to food services

Send thank you notes

Make follow-up phone calls

What questions do I need to ask during my follow-up calls?

_____

_____

_____

_____

What does this mean?

_____

_____

_____

_____

Notes

Notes

Directions for Use:

Enter a name, title, and phone number in each box. The name of the manager goes in the top center box, and his or her direct reports go below. Don't be concerned that your organizational chart is perfect. You can expect to change the boxes around as you learn more about the company and who works there.

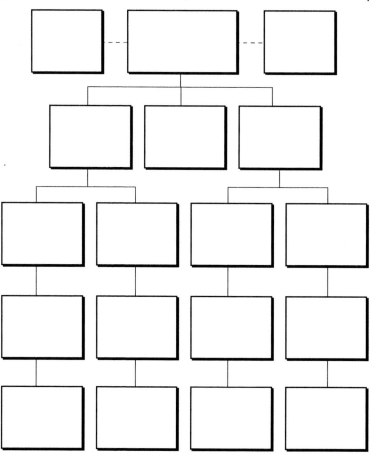

1. For whom will I be working?
2. What happened to the person I am replacing?
3. What will I be expected to accomplish?
4. Tell me about the new or upcoming products/services that you are offering.
5. By what metrics will my job performance be graded?
6. Will I have a mentor or people that I will be mentoring?
7. Tell me about the owners, directors, vice-presidents, or CEOs of this company.
8. Tell me about your competition.
9. What are you doing to be better than the competition?
10. What are your plans for growth?
11. What would my career track be?
12. How do you see the company growing over the next five years?
13. Do you like working here?
14. What are some compelling reasons to accept an offer from your company?
15. What resources are available for my position?
16. Do I have a budget and if so, how much is it?
17. When can I look forward to a performance and salary review?
18. What kind of travel is required?
19. May I get a copy of the benefits summary?
20. What relocation allowances are available?
21. What is the dress code at work?
22. Can you describe the work environment?
23. What is the desired level of production or work product?
24. What is your vision for this company or group?
25. Why are you hiring for this position?
26. What training is available?
27. What do you value in an employee?
28. What can I count on from you as my manager?
29. Do you pay for employee referrals?

30. If you could change one thing at this company, what would it be and why?
31. What types of retention programs do you have in place?
32. What is the turnover rate* for employees per year?
33. What skills and personality traits are valued at this company?

*The turnover rate is the rate at which people leave the company per year. The averages run between 10 percent and 20 percent. Lower than 10 percent is very good and higher than 30 percent is very bad. For example, a company like McDonald's has a very high turnover rate while a company like Google has a very low turnover rate. There are strong reasons for both to occur: investigate why. Check http://www.bls.gov/jlt/ for more statistical information.

Questions to Ask
After the Interview

1. How should I follow up with you?
2. How did I do in the interview?
3. When will you be making a hiring decision?
4. How many other people are you considering for this position?
5. How do I compare to those you have already interviewed for this position?
6. How long does it take for an offer to be made?
7. What are the next steps in the hiring process?
8. What is your pay schedule? (weekly, bi-weekly, monthly)
9. What kind of medical, dental, and vision insurance do you offer?
10. Do you offer tuition assistance and if so, when would that start?
11. What other benefits do you offer?
12. When will I hear if I am hired or cut from the list?

Recommended Websites

Teleconnection.com

This website offers free conference call service—a great tool for connecting with a group of professionals with whom you want to network.

Monster.com, Headhunter.com, and Yahoo.com

These are the largest employment search websites in the world. On them, you can post your resume and view listings of thousands of jobs across the country or even the world.

EEOC.gov

EEOC stands for the Equal Employment Opportunity Commission. This is the most comprehensive pool of Federal regulations on jobs. Check your local state government for other regulations as well.

DOL.gov

The United States Department of Labor can answer questions about employment regulations.

Onrec.com

This website aims to help job seekers find the best resources available to them on the Internet. It is a great place to find other job and resume posting websites that fit your specific career path.

If you are going to be taking a drug test, check these websites out. http://www.erowid.org/ Erowid documents the complex relationship between humans and psychoactive substances. http://dwp.samhsa.gov/drugtesting/dtesting.aspx Follow this link to access drug testing information on the United States Department of Health and Human Services website.

Meet Lorne in Person

I am available to travel to your hometown and give a "How to Interview" workshop to you and your community based on my book, *You're Hired! Interview Skills to Get the Job.*
I would be delighted to develop your ability to get the job you want. Contact me at Lorne@YoureHiredBook.com.